Addresses

Addresses

HENRY DRUMMOND

Arranged by ELIZABETH CURETON

ARC
MANOR
Rockville, MARYLAND
2008

ISBN: 978-1-60450-172-8

Published by Arc Manor
P. O. Box 10339
Rockville, md 20849-0339
www.ArcManor.com

Printed in the United States of America/United Kingdom

CONTENTS

Introductory

I was staying with a party of friends in a country house during my visit to England in 1884. On Sunday evening as we sat around the fire, they asked me to read and expound some portion of Scripture. Being tired after the services of the day, I told them to ask Henry Drummond, who was one of the party. After some urging he drew a small Testament from his hip pocket, opened it at the 13th chapter of I Corinthians, and began to speak on the subject of Love.

It seemed to me that I had never heard anything so beautiful, and I determined not to rest until I brought Henry Drummond to Northfield to deliver that address. Since then I have requested the principals of schools to have it read before the students every year. The one great need in our Christian life is love, more love to God and to each other. Would that we could all move into that Love chapter, and live there.

This volume contains, in addition to the address on Love, some other addresses which I trust will bring help and blessing to many.

D. L. MOODY.

Love:
The Greatest Thing in the World.

Every one has asked himself the great question of antiquity as of the modern world: What is the 'summum bonum'—the supreme good? You have life before you. Once only you can live it. What is the noblest object of desire, the supreme gift to covet?

We have been accustomed to be told that the greatest thing in the religious world is Faith. That great word has been the key-note for centuries of the popular religion; and we have easily learned to look upon it as the greatest thing in the world. Well, we are wrong. If we have been told that, we may miss the mark. In the 13th chapter of I Corinthians, Paul takes us to Christianity at its source; and there we see, "the greatest of these is love."

It is not an oversight. Paul was speaking of faith just a moment before. He says, "If I have all faith, so that I can remove mountains, and have not love, I am nothing." So far from forgetting, he deliberately contrasts them, "Now abideth Faith, Hope, Love," and without a moment's hesitation the decision falls, "The greatest of these is Love."

And it is not prejudice. A man is apt to recommend to others his own strong point. Love was not Paul's strong point. The observing student can detect a beautiful tenderness growing and ripening all through his character as Paul gets old; but the hand that wrote "The greatest of these is love," when we meet it first, is stained with blood.

Nor is this letter to the Corinthians peculiar in singling out love as the "summum bonum." The masterpieces of Christianity are agreed about it. Peter says, "Above all things have fervent love among yourselves." *above all things*. And John goes farther, "God is love."

You remember the profound remark which Paul makes elsewhere, "Love is the fulfilling of the law." Did you ever think what he meant by that? In those days men were working the passage to Heaven by keeping the Ten Commandments, and the hundred and ten other commandments which they had manufactured out of them. Christ came and said, "I will show you a more simple way. If you do one thing, you will do these hundred and ten things, without ever thinking about them. If you *love,* you will unconsciously fulfill the whole law."

You can readily see for yourselves how that must be so. Take any of the commandments. "Thou shalt have no other gods before Me." If a man love God, you will not require to tell him that. Love is the fulfilling of that law. "Take not His name in vain." Would he ever dream of taking His name in vain if he loved him? "Remember the Sabbath day to keep it holy." Would he not be too glad to have one day in seven to dedicate more exclusively to the object of his affection? Love would fulfill all these laws regarding God.

And so, if he loved man, you would never think of telling him to honor his father and mother. He could not do anything else. It would be preposterous to tell him not to kill. You could only insult him if you suggested that he should not steal—how could he steal from those he loved? It would be superfluous to beg him not to bear false witness against his neighbor. If he loved him it would be the last thing he would do. And you would never dream of urging him not to covet what his neighbors had. He would rather they possess it than himself. In this way "Love is the fulfilling of the law." It is the rule for fulfilling all rules, the new commandment for keeping all the old commandments, Christ's one.

Secret of the Christian life.

Now Paul has learned that; and in this noble eulogy he has given us the most wonderful and original account extant of the "summum bonum." We may divide it into three parts. In the beginning of the short chapter we have Love *contrasted;* in the heart of it, we have Love *analyzed;* toward the end, we have Love *defended* as the supreme gift.

I. THE CONTRAST.

Paul begins by contrasting Love with other things that men in those days thought much of. I shall not attempt to go over these things in detail. Their inferiority is already obvious.

He contrasts it with *eloquence.* And what a noble gift it is, the power of playing upon the souls and wills of men, and rousing them to lofty purpose and holy deeds! Paul says, If I speak with the tongues of men and of angels, and have not love, I am become sounding brass, or a tinkling cymbal." We all know why. We have all felt the brazenness of words without emotion, the hollowness, the unaccountable unpersuasiveness, of eloquence behind which lies no Love.

He contrasts it with *prophecy.* He contrasts it with *mysteries.* He contrasts it with *faith.* He contrasts it with *charity.* Why is Love greater than faith? Because the end is greater than the means. And why is it greater than charity? Because the whole is greater than the part.

Love is greater than *faith*, because the end is greater than the means. What is the use of having faith? It is to connect the soul with God. And what is the object of connecting man with God? That he may become like God. But God is Love. Hence Faith, the means, is in order to Love, the end. Love, therefore, obviously is greater than faith. "If I have all faith, so as to remove mountains, but have not love, I am nothing."

It is greater than *charity,* again, because the whole is greater than a part. Charity is only a little bit of Love, one of the innumerable avenues of Love, and there may even be, and there is, a great deal of charity without Love. It is a very easy thing to toss a copper to a beggar on the street; it is generally an easier thing than not to do it. Yet Love is just as often in the withholding. We purchase relief from the sympathetic feelings roused by the spectacle of misery, at the copper's cost. It is too cheap—too cheap for us, and often too dear for the beggar. If we really loved him we would either do more for him, or less. Hence, "If I bestow all my goods to feed the poor, but have not love it profiteth me nothing."

Then Paul contrasts it with *sacrifice* and martyrdom: "If I give my body to be burned, but have not love, it profiteth me nothing." Missionaries can take nothing greater to the heathen world than the impress and reflection of the Love of God upon their own character. That is the universal language. It will take them years to speak in Chinese, or in the dialects of India. From the day they land, that language of Love, understood by all, will be pouring forth its unconscious eloquence.

It is the man who is the missionary, it is not his words. His character is his message. In the heart of Africa, among the great Lakes, I have come across black men and women who remembered the only white man they ever saw before—David Livingstone; and as you cross his footsteps in that dark continent, men's faces light up as they speak of the kind doctor who passed there years ago. They could not understand him; but they felt the love that beat in his heart. They knew that it was love, although he spoke no word.

Take into your sphere of labor, where you also mean to lay down your life, that simple charm, and your life-work must succeed. You can take nothing greater, you need take nothing less. You may take every accomplishment; you may be braced for every sacrifice; but if you give your body to be burned, and have not Love, it will profit you and the cause of Christ *nothing*.

II. THE ANALYSIS

After contrasting Love with these things, Paul, in three verses, very short, gives us an amazing analysis of what this supreme thing is.

I ask you to look at it. It is a compound thing, he tells us. It is like light. As you have seen a man of science take a beam of light and pass it through a crystal prism, as you have seen it come out on the other side of the prism broken up into its component colors—red, and blue, and yellow, and violet, and orange, and all the colors of the rainbow—so Paul passes this thing, Love, through the magnificent prism of his inspired intellect, and it comes out on the other side broken up into its elements.

In these few words we have what one might call *the spectrum of Love,* the analysis of love. Will you observe what its elements are? Will you notice that they have common names; that they are virtues which we hear about every day; that they are things which can be practised by every man in every place in life; and how, by a multitude of small things and ordinary virtues, the supreme thing, the "summum bonum," is made up?

The Spectrum of Love has nine ingredients:

Patience . . . . . "Love suffereth long."

Kindness . . . . . "And is kind."

Generosity . . . . "Love envieth not."

Humility . . . . . "Love vaunteth not itself, is no puffed up."

Courtesy . . . . . "Doth not behave itself unseemly."

Unselfishness . . "Seeketh not its own."

Good temper . . . "Is not provoked."

Guilelessness . . "Taketh not account of evil."

Sincerity . . . . Rejoiceth not in unrighteousness,

"but rejoiceth with the truth."

Patience; kindness; generosity; humility; courtesy; unselfishness; good temper; guilelessness; sincerity—these make up the supreme gift, the stature of the perfect man.

You will observe that all are in relation to men, in relation to life, in relation to the known to-day and the near to-morrow, and not to the unknown eternity. We hear much of love to God; Christ spoke much of love to man. We make a great deal of peace with heaven; Christ made much of peace on earth. Religion is not a strange or added thing, but the inspiration of the secular life, the breathing of an eternal spirit through this temporal world. The supreme thing, in short, is not a thing at all, but the giving of a further finish to the multitudinous words and acts which make up the sum of every common day.

PATIENCE. This is the normal attitude of love; Love passive, love waiting to begin; not in a hurry; calm; ready to do its work when the summons comes, but meantime wearing the ornament of a meek and quiet spirit. Love suffers long; beareth all things; believeth all things; hopeth all things. For Love understands, and therefore waits.

KINDNESS. Love active. Have you ever noticed how much of Christ's life was spent in doing kind things—in merely doing kind things? Run over it with that in view, and you will find that He spent a great proportion of His time simply in making people happy, in doing good turns to people. There is only one thing greater than happiness in the world, and that is holiness; and it is not in our keeping; but what God *has* put in our power is the happiness of those about us, and that is largely to be secured by our being kind to them.

"The greatest thing," says some one, "a man can do for his Heavenly Father is to be kind to some of His other children." I wonder why it is that we are not all kinder than we are? How much the world needs it! How easily it is done! How instantaneously it acts! How infallibly it is remembered! How superabundantly it pays itself back—for there is no debtor in the world so honorable, so superbly honorable, as Love. "Love never faileth." Love is success, Love is happiness, Love is life. "Love," I say with Browning, "is energy of life."

> *"For life, with all it yields of joy or woe*
> *And hope and fear,*
> *Is just our chance o' the prize of learning love,—*
> *How love might be, hath been indeed, and is."*

Where Love is, God is. He that dwelleth in Love dwelleth in God. God is Love. Therefore *love*. Without distinction, without calculation, without procrastination, love. Lavish it upon the poor, where it is very easy; especially upon the rich, who often need it most; most of all upon our equals, where it is very difficult, and for whom perhaps we each do least of all. There is a difference between *trying to please and giving pleasure*. Give pleasure. Lose no chance of giving pleasure; for that is the ceaseless and anonymous triumph of a truly loving spirit. "I shall pass through this world but once. Any good thing, therefore, that I can do, or any kindness that I can show to any human being, let me do it now. Let me not defer it or neglect it, for I shall not pass this way again."

GENEROSITY. "Love envieth not." This is love in competition with others. Whenever you attempt a good work you will find other men doing the same kind of work, and probably doing it better. Envy them not. Envy is a feeling of ill-will to those who are in the same line as ourselves, a spirit of covetousness and detraction. How little Christian work even is a protection against un-Christian feeling! That most despicable of all the unworthy moods which cloud a Christian's soul assuredly waits for us on the threshold of every work, unless we are fortified with this grace of magnanimity. Only one thing truly need the Christian envy—the large, rich, generous soul which "envieth not."

And then, after having learned all that, you have to learn this further thing, HUMILITY—to put a seal upon your lips and forget what you have done. After you have been kind, after Love has stolen forth into the world and done its beautiful work, go back into the shade again and say nothing about it. Love hides even from itself. Love waives even self-satisfaction. "Love vaunteth not itself, is not puffed up." Humility—love hiding.

The fifth ingredient is a somewhat strange one to find in this "summum bonum:" COURTESY. This is Love in society, Love in relation to etiquette. "Love doe not behave itself unseemly."

Politeness has been defined as love in trifles. Courtesy is said to be love in little things. And the one secret of politeness is to love.

Love *cannot* behave itself unseemly. You can put the most untutored persons into the highest society, and if they have a reservoir of Love in their hearty they will not behave themselves unseemly. They simply cannot do it. Carlisle said of Robert Burns that there was no truer gentleman in Europe than the ploughman-poet. It was because he loved everything—the mouse, and the daisy, and all the things, great and small, that God had made. So with this simple passport he could mingle with any society, and enter courts and palaces from his little cottage on the banks of the Ayr.

You know the meaning of the word "gentleman." It means a gentle man—a man who does things gently, with love. That is the whole art and mystery of it. The gentle man cannot in the nature of things do an un-gentle, an ungentlemanly thing. The ungentle soul, the inconsiderate, unsympathetic nature, cannot do anything else. "Love doth not behave itself unseemly."

UNSELFISHNESS. "Love seeketh not her own." Observe: Seeketh not even that which is her own. In Britain the Englishman is devoted, and rightly, to his rights. But there come times when a man may exercise even the higher right of giving up his rights.

Yet Paul does not summon us to give up our rights. Love strikes much deeper. It would have us not seek them at all, ignore them, eliminate the personal element altogether from our calculations.

It is not hard to give up our rights. They are often eternal. The difficult thing is to give up *ourselves*. The more difficult thing still is not to seek things for ourselves at all. After we have sought them, bought them, won them, deserved them, we have taken the cream off them for ourselves already. Little cross then to give them up. But not to seek them, to look every man not on his own things, but on the things of others—that is the difficulty. "Seekest thou great things for thyself?" said the prophet; *"seek them not."* Why? Because there is no greatness in *things*. Things cannot be great. The only greatness is unselfish love. Even self-denial in itself is nothing, is almost a mistake. Only a great purpose or a mightier love can justify the waste.

It is more difficult, I have said, not to seek our own at all than, having sought it, to give it up. I must take that back. It is only true of a partly selfish heart. Nothing is a hardship to Love, and nothing is hard. I believe that Christ's "yoke" is easy. Christ's yoke is just His way of taking life. And I believe it is an easier way than any other. I believe it is a happier way than any other. The most obvious lesson in Christ's teaching is that there is no happiness in having and getting anything, but only in giving. I repeat, *there is no happiness in having or in getting, but only in giving.* Half the world is on the wrong scent in the pursuit of happiness. They think it consists in having and getting, and in being served by others. It consists in giving, and in serving others. "He that would be great among you," said Christ, "let him serve." He that would be happy, let him remember that there is but one way—"it is more blessed, it is more happy, to give than to receive."

The next ingredient is a very remarkable one: GOOD TEMPER. "Love is not provoked."

Nothing could be more striking than to find this here. We are inclined to look upon bad temper as a very harmless weakness. We speak of it as a mere infirmity of nature, a family failing, a matter of temperament, not a thing to take into very serious account in estimating a man's character. And yet here, right in the heart of this analysis of love, it finds a place; and the Bible again and again returns to condemn it as one of the most destructive elements in human nature.

The peculiarity of ill temper is that it is the vice of the virtuous. It is often the one blot on an otherwise noble character. You know men who are all but perfect, and women who would be entirely perfect, but for an easily ruffled, quick-tempered, or "touchy" disposition. This compatibility of ill temper with high moral character is one of the strangest and saddest problems of ethics. The truth is, there are two great classes of sins—sins of the *body* and sins of the *disposition*. The Prodigal Son may be taken as a type of the first, the Elder Brother of the second. Now, society has no doubt whatever as to which of these is the worse. Its brand falls, without a challenge, upon the Prodigal. But are we right? We have no balance to weigh one another's sins, and coarser and finer are but human words; but faults in the higher nature may be less venal than those in the lower, and to the eye of Him who is Love, a sin against Love may seem a hundred times more base. No form of vice, not worldliness, not greed of gold, not drunkenness itself, does more to un-Christianize society than evil temper. For embittering life, for breaking up communities, for destroying the most sacred relationships, for devastating homes, for withering up men and women, for taking the bloom of childhood, in short, for sheer gratuitous misery-producing power this influence stands alone.

Look at the Elder Brother—moral, hard-working, patient, dutiful—let him get all credit for his virtues—look at this man, this baby, sulking outside his own father's door. "He was angry," we read, "and would not go in." Look at the effect upon the father, upon the servants, upon the happiness of the guests. Judge of the effect upon the Prodigal—and how many prodigals are kept out of the Kingdom of God by the unlovely character of those who profess to be inside. Analyze, as a study in Temper, the thunder-cloud itself as it gathers upon the Elder Brother's brow. What is it made of? Jealousy, anger, pride, uncharity, cruelty, self-righteousness, touchiness, doggedness, sullenness—these are the ingredients of this dark and loveless soul. In varying proportions, also, these are the ingredients of all ill temper. Judge if such sins are of the disposition are not worse to live in, and for others to live with, than the sins of the body. Did Christ indeed not answer the question Himself when He said, "I say unto you that the publicans and the harlots go into the Kingdom of Heaven before you"? There is really no place in heaven for a disposition like this. A man with such a mood could only make heaven miserable for all the people in it. Except, therefore, such a man be born again,he cannot, simply cannot, enter the kingdom of heaven.

You will see then why Temper is significant. It is not in what it is alone, but in what it reveals. This is why I speak of it with such unusual plainness. It is a test for love, a symptom, a revelation of an unloving nature at bottom. It is the intermittent fever which bespeaks unintermittent disease within; the occasional bubble escaping to the surface which betrays some rottenness underneath; a sample of the most hidden products of the soul dropped involuntarily when off one's guard; in a word, the lightning form of a hundred hideous and un-Christian sins. A want of patience, a want of kindness, a want of generosity, a want of courtesy, a want of unselfishness, are all instantaneously symbolized in one flash of Temper.

Hence it is not enough to deal with the Temper. We must go to the source, and change the inmost nature, and the angry humors will die away of themselves. souls are made sweet not by taking the acid fluids out, but by putting something in—a great Love, a new Spirit, the Spirit of Christ. Christ, the Spirit of Christ, interpenetrating ours, sweetens, purifies, transforms all. This only can eradicate what is wrong, work a chemical change, renovate and regenerate, and rehabilitate the inner man. Will-power does not change men. Time does not change men. *Christ does.* Therefore, "Let that mind be in you which was also in Christ Jesus."

Some of us have not much time to lose. Remember, once more, that this is a matter of life or death. I cannot help speaking urgently, for myself, for yourselves. "Whoso shall offend one of these little ones, which believe in me, it were better for him that a millstone were hanged about his neck, and that he were drowned in the depth of the sea." That is to say, it is the deliberate verdict of the Lord Jesus that it is better not to live than not to love. *it is better not to live than not to love.*

GUILELESSNESS and SINCERITY may be dismissed almost without a word. Guilelessness is the grace for suspicious people. The possession of it is *the great secret of personal influence.*

You will find, if you think for a moment, that the people who influence you are people who believe in you. In an atmosphere of suspicion men shrivel up; but in that atmosphere they expand, and find encouragement and educative fellowship.

It is a wonderful thing that here and there in this hard, uncharitable world there should still be left a few rare souls who think no evil. this is the great unworldliness. Love "thinketh no evil," imputes no motive, sees the bright side, puts the best construction on every action. What a delightful state of mind to live in! What a stimulus and benediction even to meet with it for a day! To be trusted is to be saved. And if we try to influence or elevate others, we shall soon see that success is in proportion to their belief of our belief in them. The respect of another is the first restoration of the self-respect a man has lost; our ideal of what he is becomes to him the hope and pattern of what he may become.

"Love rejoiceth not in unrighteousness, but rejoiceth with the truth." I have called this *sincerity* from the words rendered in the Authorized Version by "rejoiceth in the truth." And, certainly, were this the real translation, nothing could be more just; for he who loves will love Truth not less than men. He will rejoice in the Truth—rejoice not in what he has been taught to believe; not in this church's doctrine or in that; not in this ism or in that ism; but "in *the truth*." He will accept only what is real; he will strive to get at facts; he will search for *truth* with a humble and unbiased mind, and cherish whatever he finds at any sacrifice. But the more literal translation of the Revised Version calls for just such a sacrifice for truth's sake here. For what Paul really meant is, as we there read, "Rejoiceth not in unrighteousness, but rejoiceth with the truth," a quality which probably no one English word—and certainly not *sincerity*—adequately defines. It includes, perhaps more strictly, the self-restraint which refuses to make capital out of others' faults; the charity which delights not in exposing the weakness of others, but "covereth all things"; the sincerity of purpose which endeavors to see things as they are, and rejoices to find them better than suspicion feared or calumny denounced.

So much for the analysis of Love. Now the business of our lives is to have these things fitted into our characters. That is the supreme work to which we need to address ourselves in this world, to learn Love. Is life not full of opportunities for learning Love? Every man and woman every day has a thousand of them. The world is not a playground; it is a schoolroom. Life is not a holiday, but an education. And the one eternal lesson for us all is *how better we can love.*

What makes a man a good cricketer? Practice. What makes a man a good artist, a good sculptor, a good musician? Practice. What makes a man a good linguist, a good stenographer? Practice. What makes a man a good man? Practice. Nothing else. There is nothing capricious about religion. We do not get the soul in different ways, under different laws, from those in which we get the body and the mind. If a man does not exercise his arm he develops no biceps muscle; and if a man does not exercise his soul, he acquires no muscle in his soul, no strength of character, no vigor of moral fibre, no beauty of spiritual growth. Love is not a thing of enthusiastic emotion. It is a rich, strong, manly, vigorous expression of the whole round Christian character—the Christlike nature in its fullest development. And the constituents of this great character are only to be built up by ceaseless practice.

What was Christ doing in the carpenter's shop? Practising. Though perfect, we read that he *learned* obedience, and grew in wisdom and in favor with God. Do not quarrel, therefore, with your lot in life. Do not complain of its never-ceasing cares, its petty environment, the vexations you have to stand, the small and sordid souls you have to live and work with. Above all, do not resent temptation; do not be perplexed because it seems to thicken round you more and more, and ceases neither for effort nor for agony nor prayer. That is your practice. That is the practice which god appoints you; and it is having its work in making you patient, and humble, and generous, and unselfish, and kind, and courteous. Do not grudge the hand that is moulding the still too shapeless image within you. It is growing more beautiful, though you see it not; and every touch of temptation may add to its perfection. Therefore keep in the midst of life. Do not isolate yourself. Be among men and among things, and among troubles, and difficulties, and obstacles. You remember Goethe's words: "Talent develops itself in solitude; character in the stream of life." Talent develops itself in solitude—the talent of prayer, of faith, of meditation, of seeing the unseen; character grows in the stream of the world's life. That chiefly is where men are to learn love.

How? Now, how? To make it easier, I have named a few of the elements of love. But these are only elements. Love itself can never be defined. Light is a something more than the sum of its ingredients—a glowing, dazzling, tremulous ether. And love is something more than all its elements—a palpitating, quivering, sensitive, living thing. By synthesis of all the colors, men can make whiteness, they cannot make light. By synthesis of all the virtues, men can make virtue, they cannot make love. How then are we to have this transcendent living whole conveyed into our souls? We brace our wills to secure it. We try to copy those who have it. We lay down rules about it. We watch. We pray. But these things alone will not bring love into our nature. Love is an *effect.* And only as we fulfill the right condition can we have the effect produced. Shall I tell you what the *cause* is?

If you turn to the Revised Version of the First Epistle of John you find these words: "We love because He first loved us." "We love," not "We love *him.*" That is the way the old version has it, and it is quite wrong. "*we love*—because He first loved us." Look at that word "because." It is the *cause* of which I have spoken. "*because* He first loved us," the effect follows that we love, we love Him, we love all men. We cannot help it. Because He loved us, we love, we love everybody. Our heart is slowly changed. contemplate the love of Christ, and you will love. Stand before that mirror, reflect Christ's character, and you will be changed into the same image from tenderness to tenderness. There is no other way. You cannot love to order. You can only look at the lovely object, and fall in love with it, and grow into likeness to it. And so look at this Perfect Character, this Perfect Life. Look at the great sacrifice as He laid down Himself, all through life, and upon the Cross of Calvary; and you must love Him. And loving Him, you must become like Him. Love begets love. It is a process of induction. Put a piece of Iron in the presence of an electrified body, and that piece of iron for a time becomes electrified. It is changed into a temporary magnet in the mere presence of a permanent magnet, and as long as you leave the two side by side, they are both magnets alike. Remain side by side with Him who loved us, and gave himself for us, and you, too, will become a permanent magnet, a permanently attractive force; and like Him you will draw all men unto you, like Him you will be drawn unto all men. that is the inevitable effect of Love. Any man who fulfills that cause must have that effect produced in him.

Try to give up the idea that religion comes to us by chance, or by mystery, or by caprice. It comes to us by natural law, or by supernatural law, for all law is Divine.

Edward Irving went to see a dying boy once, and when he entered the room he just put his hand on the sufferer's head, and said, "My boy, God loves you," and went away. The boy started from his bed, and called out to the people in the house, "God loves me! God loves me!"

One word! It changed that boy. The sense that God loved him overpowered him, melted him down, and began the creating of a new heart in him. And that is how the love of God melts down the unlovely heart in man, and begets in him the new creature, who is patient and humble and gentle and unselfish. And there is no other way to get it. There is no mystery about it. We love others, we love everybody, we love our enemies, *because he first loved us.*

III. THE DEFENCE.

Now I have a closing sentence or two to add about Paul's reason for singling out love as the supreme possession.

It is a very remarkable reason. In a single word it is this: *it lasts.* "Love," urges Paul, "never faileth." Then he begins again one of his marvelous lists of the great things of the day, and exposes them one by one. He runs over the things that men thought were going to last, and shows that they are all fleeting, temporary, passing away.

"Whether there be *prophecies,* they shall be done away." It was the mother's ambition for her boy in those days that he should become a prophet. For hundreds of years God had never spoken by means of any prophet, and at that time the prophet was greater than the king. Men waited wistfully for another messenger to come, and hung upon his lips when he appeared, as upon the very voice of God. Paul says, "Whether there be prophecies, they shall fail." The Bible is full of prophecies. One by one they have "failed"; that is, having been fulfilled, their work is finished; they have nothing more to do now in the world except to feed a devout man's faith.

Then Paul talks about *tongues*. That was another thing that was greatly coveted. "Whether there be tongues, they shall cease." As we all know, many, many centuries have passed since tongues have been known in this world. They have ceased. Take it in any sense you like. Take it, for illustration merely, as languages in general—a sense which was not in Paul's mind at all, and which though it cannot give us the specific lesson, will point the general truth. Consider the words in which these chapters were written—Greek. It has gone. Take the Latin—the other great tongue of those days. It ceased long ago. Look at the Indian language. It is ceasing. The language of Wales, of Ireland, of the Scottish Highlands is dying before our eyes. The most popular book in the English tongue at the present time, except the bible, is one of Dickens' works, his "Pickwick Papers." It is largely written in the language of London street-life; and experts assure us that in fifty years it will be unintelligible to the average English reader.

Then Paul goes farther, and with even greater boldness adds, "Whether there by *knowledge,* it shall be done away." The wisdom of the ancients, where is it? It is wholly gone. A schoolboy to-day knows more than Sir Isaac Newton knew; his knowledge has vanished away. You put yesterday's newspaper in the fire: its knowledge has vanished away. You buy the old editions of the great encyclopaedias for a few cents: their knowledge has vanished away. Look how the coach has been superseded by the use of steam. Look how electricity has superseded that, and swept a hundred almost new inventions into oblivion. One of the greatest living authorities, Sir William Thompson, said in Scotland, at a meeting at which I was present, "The steam-engine is passing away." "Whether there be knowledge, it shall vanish away." At every workshop you will see, in the back yard, a heap of old iron, a few wheels, a few levers, a few cranks, broken and eaten with rust. Twenty years ago that was the pride of the city. Men flocked in from the country to see the great invention; not it is superseded, its day is done. And all the boasted science and philosophy of this day will soon be old.

In my time, in the university of Edinburgh, the greatest figure in the faculty was Sir James Simpson, the discoverer of choloform. Recently his successor and nephew, Professor Simpson, was asked by the librarian of the University to go to the library and pick out the books on his subject (midwifery) that were no longer needed. His reply to the librarian was this:

"Take every text-book that is more than ten years old and put it down in the cellar."

Sir James Simpson was a great authority only a few years ago: men came from all parts of the earth to consult him; and almost the whole teaching of that time is consigned by the science of to-day to oblivion. And in every branch of science it is the same. "Now we know in part. We see through a glass darkly." Knowledge does not last.

Can you tell me anything that is going to last? Many things Paul did not condescend to name. He did not mention money, fortune, fame; but he picked out the great things of his time, the things the best men thought had something in them, and brushed them peremptorily aside. Paul had no charge against these things in themselves. All he said about them was that they would not last. They were great things, but not supreme things. There were things beyond them. What we are stretches past what we do, beyond what we possess. Many things that men denounce as sins are not sins; but they are temporary. And that is a favorite argument of the New Testament. John says of the world, not that it is wrong, but simply that it "passeth away." There is a great deal in the world that is delightful and beautiful; there is a great deal in it that is great and engrossing; but it will not last.

All that is in the world, the lust of the eye, the lust of the flesh, and the pride of life, are but for a little while. Love not the world therefore. Nothing that it contains is worth the life and consecration of an immortal soul. The immortal soul must give itself to something that is immortal. And the only immortal things are these: "Now abideth faith, hope, love, but the greatest of these is love."

Some think the time may come when two of these three things will also pass away—faith into sight, hope into fruition. Paul does not say so. We know but little now about the conditions of the life that is to come. But what is certain is that Love must last. God, the Eternal God, is Love. Covet, therefore, that everlasting gift, that one thing which it is certain is going to stand, that one coinage which will be current in the Universe when all the other coinages of all the nations of the world shall be useless and unhonored. You will give yourself to many things, give yourself first to Love. Hold things in their proportion. *hold things in their proportion*. Let at least the first great object of our lives be to achieve the character defended in these words, the character—and it is he character of Christ— which is built round Love.

I have said this thing is eternal. Did you ever notice how continually John associates love and faith with eternal life? I was not told when I was a boy that "God so loved the world that He gave His only-begotten Son, that whosoever believeth in Him should have everlasting life." What I was told, I remember, was, that God so loved the world that, if I trusted in Him, I was to have a thing called peace, or I was to have rest, or I was to have joy, or I was to have safety. But I had to find out for myself that whosoever trusteth in Him—that is, whosoever loveth Him, for trust is only the avenue to Love—hath everlasting life.

The Gospel offers a man a life. Never offer a man a thimbleful of Gospel. Do not offer them merely joy, or merely peace, or merely rest, or merely safety; tell them how Christ came to give men a more abundant life than they have, a life abundant in love, and therefore abundant in salvation for themselves, and large in enterprise for the alleviation and redemption of the world. Then only can the Gospel take hold of the whole of a man, body, soul and spirit, and give to each part of his nature its exercise and reward. Many of the current Gospels are addressed only to a part of man's nature. They offer peace, not life; faith, not Love; justification, not regeneration. And men slip back again from such religion because it has never really held them. Their nature was not all in it. It offered no deeper and gladder life-current than the life that was lived before. Surely it stands to reason that only a fuller love can compete with the love of the world.

To love abundantly is to live abundantly, and to love forever is to live forever. Hence, eternal life is inextricably bound up with love. We want to live forever for the same reason that we want to live to-morrow. Why do we want to live to-morrow? Is it because there is some one who loves you, and whom you want to see to-morrow, and be with, and love back? There is no other reason why we should live on than that we love and are beloved. It is when a man has no one to love him that he commits suicide. So long as he has friends, those who love him and whom he loves, he will live, because to live is to love. Be it but the love of a dog, it will keep him in life; but let that go, he has no contact with life, no reason to live. He dies by his own hand.

Eternal life also is to know God, and God is love. This is Christ's own definition. Ponder it. "This is life eternal, that they might know Thee the only true God, and Jesus Christ whom Thou hast sent." Love must be eternal. It is what God is. On the last analysis, then, love is life. Love never faileth, and life never faileth, so long as there is love. That is the philosophy of what Paul is showing us; the reason why in the nature of things love should be the supreme thing—because it is going to last; because in the nature of things it is an Eternal Life. It is a thing that we are living now, not that we get when we die; that we shall have a poor chance of getting when we die unless we are living now.

No worse fate can befall a man in this world than to live and grow old alone, unloving and unloved. To be lost is to live in an unregenerate condition, loveless and unloved; and to be saved is to love; and he that dwelleth in love dwelleth already in God. For God is Love.

Now I have all but finished. How many of you will join me in reading this chapter once a week for the next three months? A man did that once and it changed his whole life. Will you do it? It is for the greatest thing in the world. You might begin by reading it every day, especially the verses which describe the perfect character. "Love suffereth long, and is kind; love envieth not; love vaunteth not itself." Get these ingredients into your life. Then everything that you do is eternal. It is worth doing. It is worth giving time to. No man can become a saint in his sleep; and to fulfill the condition required demands a certain amount of prayer and meditation and time, just as improvement in any direction, bodily or mental, requires preparation and care. Address yourselves to that one thing; at any cost have this transcendent character exchanged for yours.

You will find as you look back upon your life that the moments that stand out, the moments when you have really lived, are the moments when you have done things in a spirit of love. As memory scans the past, above and beyond all the transitory pleasures of life, there leap forward those supreme hours when you have been enabled to do unnoticed kindnesses to those round about you, things too trifling to speak about, but which you feel have entered into your eternal life. I have seen almost all he beautiful things God has made; I have enjoyed almost every pleasure that He has planned for man; and yet as I look back I see standing out above all the life that has gone four or five short experiences, when the love of God reflected itself in some poor imitation, some small act of love of mine, and these seem to be the things which alone of all one's life abide. Everything else in all our lives is transitory. Every other good is visionary. But the acts of love which no man knows about, or can ever know about—they never fail.

In the book of Matthew, where the Judgement Day is depicted for us in the imagery of One seated upon a throne and dividing the sheep from the goats, the test of a man then is not, "How have I believed?" but "How have I loved?" The test of religion, the final test of religion, is not religiousness, but Love. I say the final test of religion at that great Day is not religiousness, but Love; not what I have done, not what I have believed, not what I have achieved, but how I have discharged the common charities of life. Sins of commission in that awful indictment are not even referred to. By what we have not done, *by sins of omission,* we are judged. It could not be otherwise. For the withholding of love is the negation of the spirit of Christ, the proof that we never knew Him, that for us He lived in vain. It means that He suggested nothing in all our thoughts, that He inspired nothing in all our lives, that we were not once near enough to Him to be seized with the spell of His compassion for the world. It means that—

> *"I lived for myself, I thought for myself,*
> *For myself, and none beside—*
> *Just as if Jesus had never lived,*
> *As if He had never died."*

Thank God the Christianity of today is coming nearer the world's need. Live to help that on. Thank God men know better, by a hair's breadth, what religion is, what God is, who Christ is, where Christ is. Who is Christ? He who fed the hungry, clothed the naked, visited the sick. And where is Christ? Where?—"Whoso shall receive a little child in My name receiveth Me.' And who are Christ's? "Every one that loveth is born of God."

Lessons from the Angelus.

God often speaks to men's souls through music; He also speaks to us through art. Millet's famous painting entitled "The Angelus" is an illuminated text, upon which I am going to say a few words to you to-night.

There are three things in this picture—a potato field, a country lad and a country girl standing in the middle of it, and on the far horizon the spire of a village church. That is all there is to it—no great scenery and no picturesque people. In Roman Catholic countries at the evening hour the church bell rings out to remind the people to pray. Some go into the church, while those that are in the fields bow their heads for a few moments in silent prayer.

That picture contains the three great elements which go to make up a perfectly rounded Christian life. It is not enough to have the "root of the matter" in us, but that we must be whole and entire, lacking nothing. The Angelus may bring to us suggestions as to what constitutes a complete life.

I. *The first element in a symmetrical life is work.*

Three-fourths of our time is probably spent in work. Of course the meaning of it is that our work should be just as religious as our worship, and unless we can work for the glory of God three-fourths of life remains unsanctified.

The proof that work is religious is that most of Christ's life was spent in work. During a large part of the first thirty years of His life He worked with the hammer and the plane, making ploughs and yokes and household furniture. Christ's public ministry occupied only about two and a half years of His earthly life; the great bulk of His time was simply spent in doing common everyday tasks, and ever since then work has had a new meaning.

When Christ came into the world He was revealed to three deputations who went to meet and worship Him. First came the shepherds, or working class; second, the wise men, or student class; and third, the two old people in the temple, Simeon and Anna; that is to say, Christ is revealed to men at their work, He is revealed to men at their books, and He is revealed to men at their worship. It was the old people who found Christ at their worship, and as we grow older we will spend more time exclusively in worship than we are able to do now. In the mean time we must combine our worship with our work, and we may expect to find Christ at our books and in our common task.

Why should God have provided that so many hours of every day should be occupied with work? It is because work makes men.

A university is not merely a place for making scholars, it is a place for making Christians. A farm is not a place for growing corn, it is a place for growing character, and a man has no character except that which is developed by his life and thought. God's Spirit does the building through the acts which a man performs from day to day. A student who cons out every word in his Latin and Greek instead of consulting a translation finds that honesty is translated into his character.

If he works out his mathematical problems thoroughly, he not only becomes a mathematician, but becomes a thorough man. It is by constant and conscientious attention to daily duties that thoroughness and conscientiousness and honorableness are imbedded in our beings. Character is the music of the soul, and is developed by exercise. Active use of the power entrusted to us is one of the chief means which God employs for producing the Christian graces. Hence the religion of a student demands that he be true to his work, and that he let his Christianity be shown to his fellow students and to his professors by the integrity and the conscientiousness of his academic life. A man who is not faithful in that which is least will not be faithful in that which is great. I have known men who struggled unsuccessfully for years to pass their examinations who, when they became Christians, found a new motive for work and thus were able to succeed where previously they had failed. A man's Christianity comes out as much in his work as in his worship.

Our work is not only to be done thoroughly, but it is to be done honestly. A man is not only to be honorable in his academic relations, but he must be honest with himself and in his attitude toward the truth. Students are not entitled to dodge difficulties, they must go down to the foundation principles. Perhaps the truths which are dear to us go down deeper even than we think, and we will get more out of them if we dig down for the nuggets than we will if we only pick up those that are on the surface. Other theories may perhaps be found to have false bases; if so, we ought to know it. It is well to take our surroundings in every direction to see if there is deep water; if there are shoals we ought to find out where they are. Therefore, when we come to difficulties, let us not jump lightly over them, but let us be honest as seekers after truth.

It may not be necessary for people in general to sift the doctrines of Christianity for themselves, but a student is a man whose business it is to think, to exercise the intellect which God has given him in finding out the truth. Faith is never opposed to reason, thought it is sometimes supposed by Bible teachers that it is; but you will find it is not. Faith is opposed to sight, but not to reason, thought it is not limited to reason. In employing his intellect in the search for truth a student is drawing nearer to the Christ who said, "I am the way, the truth and the life." We talk a great deal about Christ as the way and Christ as the life, but there is a side of Christ especially for the student: "I am the truth," and every student ought to be a truth-lover and a truth-seeker for Christ's sake.

II. *Another element in life, which of course is first in importance, is God.*

The Angelus is perhaps the most religious picture painted this century. You cannot look at it and see that young man standing in the field with his hat off and the girl opposite him with her hands clasped and her head bowed on her breast, without feeling a sense of God.

Do we carry about with us the thought of God wherever we go? If not, we have missed the greatest part of life. Do we have a conviction of god's abiding presence wherever we are? There is nothing more needed in this generation than a larger and more Scriptural idea of God. A great American writer has told us that when he was a boy the conception of God which he got from books and sermons was that of a wise and very strict lawyer. I remember well the awful conception of God which I had when a boy. I was given an illustrated edition of Watts' hymns, in which God was represented as a great piercing eye in the midst of a great black thunder cloud. The idea which that picture gave to my young imagination was that of

36

God as a great detective, playing the spy upon my actions, as the hymn says: *"Writing now the story of what little children do."*

That was a very mistaken and harmful idea which it has taken me years to obliterate. We think of God as "up there," or as one who made the world six thousand years ago and then retired. We must learn that He is not confined either to time or space. God is not to be thought of as merely back there in time, or up there in space. If not, where is He? "The word is nigh thee, even in thy mouth." The Kingdom of God is within you, and God Himself is among men. When are we to exchange the terrible, far-away, absentee God of our childhood for the everywhere present God of the Bible? Too many of the old Christian writers seem to have conceived of God as not much more than the greatest man—a kind of divine emperor. He is infinitely more; He is a spirit, as Jesus said to the woman at the well, and in Him we live and move and have our being. Let us think of God as Immanuel—God with us—an ever-present, omnipresent, eternal One. Long, long ago, God made matter, then He made the flowers and trees and animals, then He made man. Did He stop? Is God dead? If He lives and acts what is He doing? He is making men better.

He it is that "worketh in you." The buds of our nature are not all out yet; the sap to make them comes from the God who made us, from the indwelling Christ. Our bodies are the temples of the Holy Ghost, and we must bear this in mind, because the sense of God is kept up, not by logic, but by experience.

Until she was seven years of age the life of Helen Keller, the Boston girl who was deaf and dumb and blind, was an absolute blank; nothing could go into that mind because the ears and eyes were closed to the outer world. Then by that great process which has been discovered, by which the blind see, and the deaf hear, and the mute speak, that girl's soul became opened, and they began to put in little bits of knowledge, and bit by bit they began to educate her. They reserved her religious instruction for Phillips Brooks. After some years, when she was twelve years old, they took her to him and he began to talk to her through the young lady who could communicate with her by the exceedingly delicate process of touch. He began to tell her about God and what He had done, and how He loved men, and what He is to us. The child listened very intelligently, and finally said: "Mr. Brooks, I knew all that before, but I didn't know His name."

How often we have felt something within us impelling us to do something which we would not have conceived of by ourselves, or enabling us to do something which we could not have done alone. "It is God which worketh in you." This great simple fact explains many of the mysteries of life, and takes away the fear which we would otherwise have in meeting the difficulties which lie before us.

Two Americans who were crossing the Atlantic met on Sunday night to sing hymns in the cabin. As they sang the hymn, "Jesus, Lover of my Soul," one of the Americans heard an exceedingly rich and beautiful voice behind him. He looked around, and although he did not know the face he thought that he recognized the voice. So when the music ceased he turned and asked the man if he had not been in the Civil war. The man replied that he had been a Confederate soldier. "Were you at such a place on such a night?" asked the first. "Yes," he said, "and a curious thing happened that night; this hymn recalled it to my mind. I was on sentry duty on the edge of the wood. It was a dark night and very cold, and I was a little frightened because the enemy was supposed to be very near at hand. I felt very homesick and miserable, and about midnight, when everything was very still, I was beginning to feel very weary and thought that I would comfort myself by praying and singing a hymn. I remember singing this hymn,

'All my trust on Thee is stayed,
All my help from Thee I bring,
Cover my defenceless head
With the shadow of Thy wing.'

After I had sung those words a strange peace came down upon me, and through the long night I remember having felt no more fear."

"Now," said the other man, "listen to my story. I was a Union soldier, and was in the wood that night with a party of scouts. I saw you standing up, although I didn't see your face, and my men had their rifles focused upon you waiting the word to fire, but when you sang out,

'Cover my defenceless head
With the shadow of Thy wing.'

I said, 'Boys, put down your rifles, we will go home.' I couldn't kill you after that."

God was working in each of them, in His own way carrying out His will. God keeps his people and guides them and without Him life is but a living death.

III. *The third element in life about which I wish to speak is love.*

In this picture we notice the delicate sense of companionship, brought out by the young man and the young woman. It matters not whether they are brother and sister, or lover and loved; there you have the idea of friendship, the final ingredient in our life, after the two I have named. If the man or the woman had been standing in that field alone it would have been incomplete.

Love is the divine element in life, because "God is love." "He that loveth is born of God," therefore, as some one has said, let us "keep our friendships in repair." Let us cultivate the spirit of friendship, and let the love of Christ develop it into a great love, not only for our friends, but for all humanity. Wherever you go and whatever you do, your work will be a failure unless you have this element in your life.

These three things go far toward forming a well-rounded life. Some of us may not have these ingredients in their right proportion, but if you are lacking in one or the other of them, then pray for it and work for it that your life may be rounded and complete as God intended it should be.

Pax Vobiscum.

I once heard a sermon by a distinguished preacher upon "Rest." It was full of beautiful thoughts; but when I came to ask myself, "How does he say I can get Rest?" there was no answer. The sermon was sincerely meant to be practical, yet it contained no experience that seemed to me to be tangible, nor any advice that I could grasp—any advice, that is to say, which could help me to find the thing itself as I went about the world.

Yet this omission of what is, after all, the only important problem, was not the fault of the preacher. The whole popular religion is in the twilight here. And when pressed for really working specifics for the experiences with which it deals, it falters, and seems to lose itself in mist.

The want of connection between the great words of religion and every-day life has bewildered and discouraged all of us. Christianity possesses the noblest words in the language; its literature overflows with terms expressive of the greatest and happiest moods which can fill the soul of man. Rest, Joy, Peace, Faith, Love, Light—these words occur with such persistency in hymns and prayers that an observer might think they formed the staple of Christian experience. But on coming to close quarters with the actual life of most of us, how surely would he be disenchanted. I do not think we ourselves are aware of how much our religious life is made up of phrases; how much of what we call Christian Experience is only a dialect of the Churches, a mere religious phraseology with almost nothing behind it in what we really feel and know.

To some of us, indeed, the Christian experiences seem further away than when we took the first steps in the Christian life. That life has not opened out as we had hoped. We do not regret our religion, but we are disappointed with it. There are times, perhaps, when wandering notes form a diviner music stray into our spirits; but these experiences come at few and fitful moments. We have no sense of possession in them. When they visit us, it is as surprise. When they leave us, it is without explanation. When we wish their return, we do not know how to secure it.

All of which means a religion without solid base, and a poor and flickering life. It means a great bankruptcy in those experiences which give Christianity its personal solace and make it attractive to the world, and a great uncertainty as to any remedy. It is as if we knew everything about health—except the way to get it.

I am quite sure that the difficulty does not lie in the fact that men are not in earnest. This is simply not the fact. All around us Christians are wearing themselves out in trying to be better. The amount of spiritual longing in the world—in the hearts of unnumbered thousands of men and women in whom we should never suspect it; among the wise and thoughtful, among the young and gay, who seldom assuage and never betray their thirst—this is one of the most wonderful and touching facts of life. It is not more heart that is needed, but more light; not more force, but a wiser direction to be given to very real energies already there.

The usual advice when one asks for counsel on these questions is, "Pray." But this advice is far from adequate. I shall qualify the statement presently; but let me urge it here, with what you will perhaps call daring emphasis, that to pray for these things is not the way to get them. No one will get them without praying; but that men do not get them by praying is a simple fact. We have all prayed, and sincerely prayed, for such experiences as I have named; prayed, believing that that was the way to get them. And yet have we got them? The test is experience. I dare not limit prayer; still less the grace of God. If you have got them in this way, it is well. I am speaking to those, be they few or many, who have not got them; to ordinary men in ordinary circumstances. But if we have not got them, it by no means follows that prayer is useless. The correct conclusion is only that it is useless, or inadequate rather, for this particular purpose. To make prayer the sole resort, the universal panacea for every spiritual ill, is as radical a mistake as to prescribe only one medicine for every bodily trouble. The physician who does the last is a quack; the spiritual advisor who dies the first is grossly ignorant of his profession.

To do nothing but pray is a wrong done to prayer itself, and can only end in disaster. It is as if one tried to live only with the lungs, as if one assimilated only air and neglected solid food. The lungs are a first essential; the air is a first essential; but the body has many members, given for different purposes, secreting different things, and each has a method of nutrition as special to itself as its own activity. While prayer, then, is the characteristic sublimity of the Christian life, it is by no means the only one. And those who make it the sole alternative, and apply it to purposes for which it was never meant, are really doing the greatest harm to prayer itself. To couple the word "inadequate" with this might word is not to dethrone prayer, but to exalt it. What dethrones prayer is unanswered prayer. When men pray for things which do not come that way—pray with sincere belief that prayer, unaided and alone, will compass what they ask—then, not getting what they ask, they often give up prayer.

This is the natural history of much atheism, not only an atheism of atheists, but a more terrible atheism of Christians, an unconscious atheism, whose roots have struck far into many souls whose last breath would be spent in denying it. So, I repeat, it is a mistaken Christianity which allow men to cherish a blind belief in the omnipotence of prayer. Prayer, certainly, when the appropriate conditions are fulfilled, is omnipotent, but not blind prayer. Blind prayer is superstition. Prayer, in its true sense, contains the sane recognition that while man prays in faith, *God acts by law.* What that means in the immediate connection we shall see presently.

What, then, is the remedy? It is impossible to doubt that there is a remedy, and it is equally impossible to believe that it is a secret. The idea that some few men, by happy chance or happier temperament, have been given the secret—as if there were some sort of knack or trick of it—is wholly incredible and wrong. Religion must be for all, and the way into its loftiest heights must be by a gateway through which the peoples of the world may pass.

I shall have to lead up to this gateway by a very familiar path. But as this path is strangely unfrequented where it passes into the religious sphere, I must ask your forbearance for dwelling for a moment upon the commonest of commonplaces.

I. EFFECTS REQUIRE CAUSES

Nothing that happens in the world happens by chance. God is a God of order. Everything is arranged upon definite principles, and never at random. the world, even the religious world, is governed by law. Character is governed by law. Happiness is governed by law. The Christian experiences are governed by law. Men, forgetting this, expect Rest, Joy, Peace, Faith to drop into their souls from the air like snow or rain. But in point of fact they do not do so; and if they did, they would no less have their origin in previous activities and be controlled by natural laws. Rain and snow do drop from the air, but not without a long previous history. They are the mature effects of former causes. Equally so are Rest and Peace and Joy. They, too, have each a previous history. Storms and winds and calms are not accidents, but brought about by antecedent circumstances. Rest and Peace are but calms in man's inward nature, and arise through causes as definite and as inevitable.

Realize it thoroughly; it is a methodical, not an accidental world. If a housewife turns out a good cake, it is the result of a sound receipt, carefully applied. She cannot mix the assigned ingredients and fire them for the appropriate time without producing the result. It is not she who has made the cake; it is nature. She brings related things together; sets causes at work; these causes bring about the result. she is not a creator, but an intermediary. She does not expect random causes to produce specific effects—random ingredients would only produce random cakes. So it is in the making of Christian experiences. Certain lines are followed; certain effects are the result. These effects cannot but be the result. But the result can never take place without the previous cause. To expect results without antecedents is to expect cakes without ingredients. That impossibility is precisely the almost universal expectation.

Now what I mainly wish to do is to help you firmly to grasp this simple principle of Cause and Effect in the spiritual world. And instead of applying the principle generally to each of the Christian experiences in turn, I shall examine its application to one in some little detail. The one I shall select is Rest. And I think any one who follows the application in this single instance will be able to apply it for himself to the others.

Take such a sentence as this: African explorers are subject to fevers which cause restlessness and delirium.

Note the expression, "cause restlessness." *restlessness has a cause.* Clearly, then, any one who wished to get rid of restlessness would proceed at once to deal with the cause. If that were not removed, a doctor might prescribe a hundred things, and all might be taken in turn, without producing the least effect. Things are so arranged in the original planning of the world that certain effects must follow certain causes, and certain causes must be abolished before certain effects can be removed. Certain parts of Africa are inseparably linked with the physical experience called fever; this fever is in turn infallibly linked with a mental experience called restlessness and delirium. To abolish the mental experience the radical method would be to abolish the physical experience, and the way of abolishing the physical experience would be to abolish Africa, or to cease to go there.

Now this hold good for all other forms of Restlessness. Every other form and kind of Restlessness in the world had a definite cause, and the particular kind of Restlessness can only be removed by removing the allotted cause.

All this is also true of Rest. Restlessness has a cause: must not *rest* have a cause? Necessarily. If it were a chance world we would not expect this; but, being a methodical world, it cannot be otherwise. Rest, physical rest, moral rest, spiritual rest, every kind of rest has a cause, as certainly as restlessness. Now causes are discriminating. There is one kind of cause for every particular effect and no other, and if one particular effect is desired, the corresponding cause must be set in motion. It is no use proposing finely devised schemes, or going through general pious exercises in the hope that somehow Rest will come. The Christian life is not casual, but causal. All nature is a standing protest against the absurdity of expecting to secure spiritual effects, or any effects, without the employment of appropriate causes. The Great Teacher dealt what ought to have been the final blow to this infinite irrelevancy by a single question, "Do men gather grapes of thorns or figs of thistles?"

Why, then, did the Great Teacher not educate His followers fully? Why did He not tell us, for example, how such a thing as Rest might be obtained? The answer is that *he did.* But plainly, explicitly, in so many words? Yes, plainly, explicitly, in so many words. He assigned Rest to its cause, in words with which each of us has been familiar from his earliest childhood.

He begins, you remember—for you at once know the passage I refer to—almost as if Rest could be had without any cause; "Come unto me," He says, "and I will *give* you Rest."

Rest, apparently, was a favor to be bestowed; men had but to come to Him; He would give it to every applicant. But the next sentence takes that all back. The qualification, indeed, is added instantaneously. For what the first sentence seemed to give was next thing to an impossibility. For how, in a literal sense, can Rest be *given?* One could no more give away Rest than he could give away Laughter. We speak of "causing" laughter, which we can do; but we can not give it away. When we speak of "giving" pain, we know perfectly well we can not give pain away. And when we aim at "giving" pleasure, all that we can do is to arrange a set of circumstances in such a way as that these shall cause pleasure. Of course there is a sense, and a very wonderful sense, in which a Great Personality breathes upon all who come within its influence an abiding peace and trust. Men can be to other men as the shadow of a great rock in a weary land; much more Christ; much more Christ as Perfect Man; much more still as Savior of the world. But it is not this of which I speak. When Christ said He would give men Rest, He meant simply that he would put them in the way of it. By no act of conveyance would or could He make over His own Rest to them. He could give them his receipt for it. That was all. But He would not make it for them. For one thing it was not in His plan to make it for them; for another thing, men were not so planned that it could be made for them; and for yet another thing, it was a thousand times better that they should make it for themselves.

That this is the meaning becomes obvious from the wording of the second sentence: "Learn of me, and ye shall *find* Rest." Rest, (that is to say), is not a thing that can be *given,* but a thing to be *acquired.* It comes not by an act, but by a process. It is not to be found in a happy hour, as one finds a treasure; but slowly, as one finds knowledge. It could indeed be no more found in a moment than could knowledge. A soil has to be prepared for it. Like a fine fruit, it will grow in one climate, and not in another; at one altitude, and not at another. Like all growth it will have an orderly development and mature by slow degrees.

The nature of this slow process Christ clearly defines when He says we are to achieve Rest by *learning.* "Learn of me," He says, "and ye shall find rest to your souls."

Now consider the extraordinary originality of this utterance. how novel the connection between these two words "Learn" and "Rest." How few of us have ever associated them—ever thought that Rest was a thing to be learned; ever laid ourselves out for it as we would to learn a language; ever practised it as we would practice the violin? Does it not show how entirely new Christ's teaching still is to the world, that so old and threadbare an aphorism should still be so little known? The last thing most of us would have thought of would have been to associate *rest* with *work*.

What must one work at? What is that which if duly learned will find the soul of man in Rest? Christ answers without the least hesitation. He specifies two things—Meekness and Lowliness. "Learn of me," He says, "for I am *meek* and *lowly* in heart."

Now these two things are not chosen at random. To these accomplishments, in a special way, Rest is attached. Learn these, in short, and you have already found Rest. These as they stand direct causes of Rest; will produce it at once; cannot but produce it at once. And if you think for a single moment, you will see how this is necessarily so, for causes are never arbitrary, and the connection between antecedent and consequent her and everywhere lies deep in the nature of things.

What is the connection, then? I answer by a further question.

What are the chief causes of unrest?

If you know yourself, you will answer—Pride, Selfishness, Ambition. As you look back upon the past years of your life, is it not true that its unhappiness has chiefly come from the succession of personal mortifications and almost trivial disappointments which the intercourse of life has brought you? Great trials come at lengthened intervals, and we rise to breast them; but it is the petty friction of our every-day life with one another, the jar of business or of work, the discord of the domestic circle, the collapse of our ambition, the crossing of our will or the taking down of our conceit, which make inward peace impossible. Wounded vanity, then, disappointed hopes, unsatisfied selfishness—these are the old, vulgar, universal sources of man's unrest.

Now it is obvious why Christ pointed out as the two chief objects for attainment the exact opposites of these. To meekness and lowliness these things simply do not exist. They cure unrest by making it impossible. These remedies do not trifle with surface symptoms; they strike at once at removing causes. The ceaseless chagrin of a self-centered life can be removed at once by learning meekness and lowliness of heart. He who learns them is forever proof against it. He lives henceforth a charmed life. Christianity is a fine inoculation, a transfusion of healthy blood into an anaemic or poisoned soul. No fever can attack a perfectly sound body; no fever of unrest can disturb a soul which has breathed the air or learned the ways of Christ.

Men sigh for the wings of a dove that they may fly away and be at Rest. But flying away will not help us. "The Kingdom of God is *within you*." We aspire to the top to look for Rest; it lies at the bottom. Water rests only when it gets to the lowest place. So do men. Hence, *be lowly*. The man who has no opinion of himself at all can never be hurt if others do not acknowledge him. Hence, *be meek*. He who is without expectation cannot fret if nothing comes to him. It is self-evident that these things are so. The lowly man and the meek man are really above all other men, above all other things. They dominate the world because they do not care for it. The miser does not possess gold, gold possesses him. But the meek possess it. "The meek," said Christ, "inherit the earth." They do not buy it; they do not conquer it; but they inherit it.

There are people who go about the world looking out for slights, and they are necessarily miserable, for they find them at every turn—especially the imaginary ones. One has the same pity for such men as for the very poor. They are the morally illiterate. They have had no real education, for they have never learned how to live.

Few men know how to live. We grow up at random carrying into mature life the merely animal methods and motives which we had as little children. And it does not occur to us that all this must be changed that much of it must be reversed; that life is the finest of the Fine Arts; that it has to be learned with life-long patience, and that the years of our pilgrimage are all too short to master it triumphantly. Yet this is what Christianity is for—to teach men the art of life.

And its whole curriculum lies in one word—"Learn of me." Unlike most education, this is almost purely personal; it is not to be had from books, or lectures or creeds or doctrines. It is a study from the life. Christ never said much in mere words about the Christian graces. He lived them, He was them. Yet we do not merely copy Him. We learn His art by living with Him, like the old apprentices with their masters.

Now we understand it all? Christ's invitation to the weary and heavy-laden is a call to begin life over again upon a new principle—upon His own principle. "Watch my way of doing things," He says; "Follow me. Take life as I take it. Be meek and lowly, and you will find Rest."

I do not say, remember, that the Christian life to every man, or to any man, can be a bed of roses. No educational process can be this. And perhaps if some men knew how much was involved in the simple "learn" of Christ, they would not enter His school with so irresponsible a heart. For there is not only much to learn, but much to unlearn. Many men never go to this school at all till their disposition is already half ruined and character has taken on its fatal set. To learn arithmetic is difficult at fifty—much more to learn Christianity. To learn simply what it is to be meek and lowly, in the case of one who has had no lessons in that in childhood, may cost him half of what he values most on earth. Do we realize, for instance, that the way of teaching humility is generally by *humiliation?* There is probably no other school for it. When a man enters himself as a pupil in such a school it means a very great thing. There is much Rest there, but there is also much Work.

I should be wrong, even though my theme is the brighter side, to ignore the cross and minimize the cost. Only it gives to the cross a more definite meaning, and a rarer value, to connect it thus directly and casually with the growth of the inner life. Our platitudes on the "benefits of affliction" are usually about as vague as our theories of Christian Experience. "Somehow" we believe affliction does us good. But it is not a question of "Somehow." The result is definite, calculable, necessary. It is under the strictest law of cause and effect. The first effect of losing one's fortune, for instance, is humiliation; and the effect of humiliation, as we have just seen, is to make one humble; and the effect of being humble is to produce Rest. It is a roundabout way, apparently, of producing Rest; but Nature generally works by circular processes; and it is not certain that there is any other way of becoming humble, or of finding Rest. *If* a man could make himself humble to order, it might simplify matters; but we do not find that this happens. Hence we must all go through the mill. Hence death, death to the lower self, is the nearest gate and the quickest road to life.

Yet this is only half the truth. Christ's life outwardly was one of the most troubled lives that was ever lived: tempest and tumult, tumult and tempest, the waves breaking over it all he time till the worn body was laid in the grave. But the inner life was a sea of glass. The great calm was always there. At any moment you might have gone to Him and found Rest. Even when the blood-hounds were dogging Him in the streets of Jerusalem, He turned to His disciples and offered them, as a last legacy, "My peace." Nothing ever for a moment broke the serenity of Christ's life on earth. Misfortune could not reach Him; He had no fortune. Food, raiment, money—fountain-heads of half the world's weariness—He simply did not care for; they played no part in His life; He "took no thought" for them. It was impossible to affect Him by lowering His reputation. He had already made Himself of no reputation. He was dumb before insult. When he was reviled, He reviled not again. In fact, there was nothing that the world could do to him that could ruffle the surface of His spirit.

Such living, as mere living, is altogether unique. It is only when we see what it was in Him that we can know what the word Rest means. It lies not in emotions, or in the absence of emotions. It is not a hallowed feeling that comes over us in church. It is not something that the preacher has in his voice. It is not in nature, or in poetry, or in music—though in all these there is soothing. It is the mind at leisure from itself. It is the perfect poise of the soul; the absolute adjustment of the inward man to the stress of all outward things; the preparedness against every emergency; the stability of assured convictions; the eternal calm of an invulnerable faith; the repose of a heart set deep in God. It is the mood of the man who says, with Browning, "God's in His Heaven, all's well with the world."

Two painters each painted a picture to illustrate his conception of rest. The first chose for his scene a still lone lake among the far-off mountains. The second threw on his canvas a thundering waterfall, with a fragile birch-tree bending over the foam; at the fork of a branch, almost wet with the cataract's spray, a robin sat on its nest. The first was only *stagnation;* the last was *rest*. For in Rest there are always two elements—tranquility and energy; silence and turbulence; creation and destruction; fearlessness and fearfulness. This it was in Christ.

It is quite plain from all this that whatever else He claimed to be or to do, He at least knew how to live.

All this is the perfection of living, of living in the mere sense of passing through the world in the best way. Hence His anxiety to communicate His idea of life to others. He came, He said, to give men life, true life, a more abundant life than they were living; "the life," as the fine phrase in the Revised Version has it, "that is life indeed." This is what He Himself possessed, and it was this which He offers to mankind. And hence His direct appeal for all to come to Him who had not made much of life, who were weary and heavy-laden. These He would teach His secret. They, also, should know "the life that is life indeed."

II. WHAT YOKES ARE FOR.

There is still one doubt to clear up. After the statement, "Learn of Me," Christ throws in the disconcerting qualification: "Take My yoke upon you, and learn of Me."

Why, if all this be true, does He call it a *yoke?* Why, while professing to give Rest, does He with the next breath whisper *"burden"?* Is the Christian life, after all, what its enemies take it for—an additional weight to the already great woe of life, some extra punctiliousness about duty, some painful devotion to observances, some heavy restriction and trammeling of all that is joyous and free in the world? Is life not hard and sorrowful enough without being fettered with yet another yoke?

It is astounding how so glaring a misunderstanding of this plain sentence should ever have passed into currency. Did you ever stop to ask what a yoke is really? Is it to be a burden to the animal which wears it? It is just the opposite. It is to make its burden light. Attached to the oxen in any other way than by a yoke, the plough would be intolerable. Worked by means of a yoke, it is light. A yoke is not an instrument of torture; it is an instrument of mercy.

It is not a malicious contrivance for making work hard; it is a gentle device to make hard labor light. It is not meant to give pain, but to save pain. And yet men speak of the yoke of Christ as if it were slavery, and look upon those who wear it as objects of compassion. For generations we have had homilies on "The Yoke of Christ"—some delighting in portraying its narrow exactions; some seeking in those exactions the marks of its divinity; others apologizing for it, and toning it down; still others assuring us that, although it be very bad, it is not to be compared with the positive blessings of Christianity. How many, especially among the young, has this one mistaken phrase driven forever away from the kingdom of God? Instead of making Christ attractive, it makes Him out a taskmaster, narrowing life by petty restrictions, calling for self-denial where none is necessary, making misery a virtue under the plea that it is the yoke of Christ, and happiness criminal because it now and then evades it. According to this conception, Christians are at best the victims of a depressing fate; their life is a penance; and their hope for the next world purchased by a slow martyrdom in this.

The mistake has arisen from taking the word "yoke" here in the same sense as in the expression "under the yoke," or "wear he yoke in his youth." But in Christ's illustration it is not the "jugum" of the Roman soldier, but the simple "harness" or "ox-collar" of the Eastern peasant. It is the literal wooden yoke which He, with His own hands in the carpenter shop, had probably often made. He knew the difference between a smooth yoke and a rough one, a bad fit and a good fit; the difference also it made to the patient animal which had to wear it. The rough yoke galled, and the burden was heavy; the smooth yoke caused no pain, and the load was lightly drawn. The badly fitted harness was a misery; the well-fitted collar was "easy."

And what was the "burden"? It was not some special burden laid upon the Christian, some unique infliction that they alone must bear. It was what all men bear. It was simply life, human life itself, the general burden of life which all must carry with them from the cradle to the grave. Christ saw that men took life painfully. To some it was a weariness, to others a failure, to many a tragedy, to all a struggle and a pain. How to carry this burden of life had been the whole world's problem. It is still the whole world's problem. And here is Christ's solution: "Carry it as I do. Take life as I take it. Look at it from My point of view. Interpret it upon My principles. Take My yoke and learn of me, and you will find it easy. For my yoke is easy, works easily, sits right upon the shoulders, and *therefore* My burden is light."

There is no suggestion here that religion will absolve any man from bearing burdens. That would be to absolve him from living, since it is life itself that is the burden. What Christianity does propose is to make it tolerable. Christ's yoke is simply His secret for the alleviation of human life, His prescription for the best and happiest method of living. Men harness themselves to the work and stress of the world in clumsy and unnatural ways. The harness they put on is antiquated. A rough, ill-fitted collar at best, they make its strain and friction past enduring, by placing it where the neck is most sensitive; and by mere continuous irritation this sensitiveness increases until the whole nature is quick and sore.

This is the origin, among other things, of a disease called "touchiness"—a disease which, in spite of its innocent name, is one of the gravest sources of restlessness in the world. Touchiness, when it becomes chronic, is a morbid condition of the inward disposition. It is self-love inflamed to the acute point; conceit, *with a hair-trigger.* The cure is to shift the yoke to some other place; to let men and things touch us through some new and perhaps as yet unused part of our nature; to become meek and lowly in heart while the old sensitiveness is becoming numb from want of use.

It is the beautiful work of Christianity everywhere to adjust the burden of life to those who bear it, and them to it. It has a perfectly miraculous gift of healing. Without doing any violence to human nature it sets it right with life, harmonizing it with all surrounding things, and restoring those who are jaded with the fatigue and dust of the world to a new grace of living. In the mere matter of altering the perspective of life and changing the proportions of things, its function in lightening the care of man is altogether its own.

The weight of a load depends upon the attraction of the earth. Suppose the attraction of the earth were removed? A ton on some other planet, where the attraction of gravity is less, does not weigh half a ton. Now Christianity removes the attraction of the earth; and this is one way in which it diminishes man's burden. It makes them citizens of another world. What was a ton yesterday is not half a ton today. So without changing one's circumstances, merely by offering a wider horizon and a different standard, it alters the whole aspect of the world.

Christianity as Christ taught is the truest philosophy of life ever spoken. but let us be quite sure when we speak of Christianity that we mean Christ's Christianity. Other versions are either caricatures, or exaggerations, or misunderstandings, or shortsighted and surface readings. For the most part their attainment is hopeless and the results wretched. But I care not who the person is, or through what vale of tears he has passed, or is about to pass, there is a new life for him along this path.

III. HOW FRUITS GROW.

Were Rest my subject, there are other things I should wish to say about it, and other kinds of Rest of which I should like to speak. But that is not my subject. My theme is that the Christian experiences are not the work of magic, but come under the law of Cause and Effect. I have chosen Rest only as a single illustration of the working of that principle. If there were time I might next run over all the Christian experiences in turn, and show the same wide law applies to each; but I think it may serve the better purpose if I leave this further exercise to yourselves. I know no Bible study that you will find more full of fruit, of which will take you nearer to the ways of God, or make the Christian life itself more solid or more sure. I shall add only a single other illustration of what I mean, before I close.

Where does Joy come from? I knew a Sunday scholar whose conception of Joy was that it was a thing made in lumps and kept somewhere in Heaven, and that when people prayed for it, pieces were somehow let down and fitted into their souls. I am not sure that views as gross and material are not often held by people who ought to be wiser. In reality, Joy is as much a matter of Cause and Effect as pain. No one can get Joy by merely asking for it. It is one of the ripest fruits of the Christian life, and, like all fruits, must be grown. There is a very clever trick in India called the mango trick. A seed is put in the ground and covered up, and after diverse incantations a full-blown mango-bush appears within five minutes. I never met any one who knew how the thing was done, but I never met any one who believed it to be anything else than a conjuring trick. The world is pretty unanimous now in its belief in the orderliness of Nature. Men may not know how fruits grow, but they do know that they cannot grow in an hour. Some lives have not even a stalk on which fruits could hang, even if they did grow in an hour. Some have never planted one seed of Joy in all their lives; and others who may have planted a germ or two have lived so little in sunshine that they never could come to maturity.

Whence, then, is joy? Christ put His teaching upon this subject into one of the most exquisite of His parables. I should in any instance have appealed to His teaching here, as in the case of Rest, for I do not wish you to think I am speaking words of my own. But it so happens that He has dealt with it in words of unusual fullness.

I need not recall the whole illustration. It is the parable of the Vine. Did you ever think why Christ spoke that parable? He did not merely throw it into space as a find illustration of general truths. It was not simply a statement of the mystical union, and the doctrine of an indwelling Christ. It was that; but it was more. After He had said it, He did what was not an unusual thing when He was teaching His greatest lessons—He turned to the disciples and said He would tell them why He had spoken it. It was to tell them how to get joy.

"These things I have spoken unto you," He said, "that My Joy might remain in you, and that your Joy might be full." It was a purposed and deliberate communication of His secret of happiness.

Go back over these verses, then, and you will find the Causes of this Effect, the spring, and the only spring, out of which true Happiness comes. I am not going to analyze them in detail. I ask you to enter into the words for yourselves.

Remember, in the first place, that the Vine was the Eastern symbol of Joy. It was its fruit that made glad the heart of man. Yet, however innocent that gladness—for the expressed juice of the grape was the common drink at every peasant's board—the gladness was only a gross and passing thing. This was not true happiness, and the vine of the Palestine vineyards was not the true vine. *"christ* was the *true* Vine."* Here, then, is the ultimate source of Joy. Through whatever media it reaches us, all true Joy and Gladness find their source in Christ.

By this, of course, is not meant that the actual Joy experienced is transferred from Christ's nature, or is something passed on from Him to us. What is passed on is His method of getting it. There is, indeed, a sense in which we can share another's joy or another's sorrow. But that is another matter. Christ is the source of Joy to men in the sense in which He is the source of Rest. His people share His life, and therefore share its consequences, and one of these is Joy. His method of living is one that in the nature of things produces Joy. When He spoke of His Joy remaining with us He meant in part that the causes which produced it should continue to act. His followers, (that is to say), by *repeating* His life would experience its accompaniments. His Joy, His kind of Joy, would remain with them.

The medium through which this Joy comes is next explained: "He that abideth in Me, the same bringeth forth much fruit." Fruit first, Joy next; the one the cause or medium of the other. Fruit-bearing is the necessary antecedent; Joy both the necessary consequent and the necessary accompaniment. It lay partly in the bearing fruit, partly in the fellowship which made that possible. Partly, that is to say, Joy lay in mere constant living in Christ's presence, with all that that implied of peace, of shelter, and of love; partly in the influence of that Life upon mind and character and will; and partly in the inspiration to live and work for others, with all that that brought of self-riddance and joy in others' gain. All these, in different ways and at different times, are sources of pure happiness.

Even the simplest of them—to do good to other people—is an instant and infallible specific. There is no mystery about Happiness whatever. Put in the right ingredients and it must come out. He that abideth in Him will bring forth much fruit; and bringing forth much fruit is Happiness. The infallible receipt for Happiness, then, is to do good; and the infallible receipt for doing good is to abide in Christ. The surest proof that all this is a plain matter of Cause and Effect is that men may try every other conceivable way of finding happiness, and they will fail. Only the right cause in each case can produce the right effect.

Then the Christian experiences are our own making? In the same sense in which grapes are our own making and no more. All fruits *grow*—whether they grow in the soil or in the soul; whether they are the fruits of the wild grape or of the True Vine. No man can *make* things grow. He can *get them to grow* by arranging all the circumstances and fulfilling all the conditions. But the growing is done by God. Causes and effects are eternal arrangements, set in the constitution of the world; fixed beyond man's ordering. What man can do is to place himself in the midst of a chain of sequences. Thus he can get things to grow. But the power is the Spirit of God.

What more need I add but this—test the method by experiment. Do not imagine that you have got these things because you know how to get them. As well try to feed upon a cookery book. But I think I can promise that if you try in this simple and natural way, you will not fail. Spend the time you have spent in sighing for fruits in fulfilling the conditions of their growth. The fruits will come, must come. We have hitherto paid immense attention to *effects*, to the mere experiences themselves; we have described them, extolled them, advised them, prayed for them—done everything but find out what *caused* them. Henceforth let us deal with causes.

"To be," says Lotze, "is to be in relations." About every other method of living the Christian life there is an uncertainty. About every other method of acquiring the Christian experiences there is a "perhaps." But in so far as this method is the way of nature, it cannot fail. Its guarantee is the laws of the universe—and these are "the Hands of the Living God."

The True Vine.

"I am the true vine, and my Father is the husbandman. Every branch in me that beareth not fruit he taketh away; and every branch that beareth fruit, he purgeth it, that it may bring forth more fruit. Now ye are clean through the word which I have spoken unto you. Abide in me, and I in you. As the branch cannot bear fruit of itself, except it abide in the vine; no more can ye, except ye abide in me. I am the vine, ye are the branches: He that abideth in me, and I in him, the same bringeth forth much fruit: for without me ye can do nothing. If a man abide not in me, he is cast forth as a branch, and is withered; and men gather them, and cast them into the fire, and they are burned. If ye abide in me, and my word abide in you, ye shall ask what ye will, and it shall be done unto you. Herein is my Father glorified, that ye bear much fruit; so ye shall be my disciples. As the Father hath loved me, so have I loved you: continue ye in my love. If ye keep my commandments, ye shall abide in my love; even as I have kept my Father's commandments, and abide in his love. These things have I spoken unto you, that my joy might remain in you, and that your joy might be full."

"First!" An Address to Boys.

I have three heads to give you. The first is "Geography," the second is "Arithmetic," and the third is "Grammar."

I. *First. Geography tells us where to find places.*

Where is the Kingdom of God? It is said that when a Prussian officer was killed in the Franco-Prussian war, a map of France was very often found in his pocket. When we wish to occupy a country, we ought to know its geography. Now, *where* is the Kingdom of God? A boy over there says, "It is in heaven." No; it is not in heaven. Another boy says, "It is in the Bible." No; it is not in the Bible. Another boy says, "It must be in the Church," No; it is not in the Church. Heaven is only the capital of the Kingdom of God; the Bible is the guide-book to it; the Church is the weekly parade of those who belong to it. If you turn to the seventeenth chapter of Luke you will find out where the Kingdom of God really is: "The Kingdom of God is within you"—within *you*. The Kingdom of God is *inside people.*

I remember once taking a walk by the river near where the Falls of Niagara are, and I noticed a remarkable figure walking along the river bank. I had been some time in America. I had seen black men, and red men, and yellow men, and white men; black men, the Negroes; red men, the Indians; yellow men, the Chinese; white men, the Americans. But this man looked quite different in his dress from anything I had ever seen. When he came a little closer, I saw he was wearing a kilt; when he came a little nearer still, I saw that he was dressed exactly like a Highland soldier. When he came quiet near, I said to him: "What are you doing here?"

"Why should I not be here?" he replied; "don't you know this is British soil? When you cross the river you come into Canada."

This soldier was thousands of miles from England, and yet he was in the Kingdom of England. Wherever there is an English heart beating loyal to the Queen of Britain, there is England. Wherever there is a boy whose heart is loyal to the Kingdom of God, the Kingdom of God is within him.

What is the Kingdom of God? Every Kingdom has its exports, it products. Go down the river here and you will find ships coming in with cotton; you know they come from America. You will find ships with tea; you know they are from China. Ships with wool; you know they come from Australia. Ships with sugar; you know they come from Java.

What comes from the Kingdom of God? Again, we must refer to our Guide-book. Turn to Romans, and we shall find what the Kingdom of God is. I will read it: "The Kingdom of God is righteousness, peace, joy"— three things. "The Kingdom of God is righteousness, peace, joy." Righteousness, of course is just doing what is right. Any boy who does what is *right* has the Kingdom of God within him. Any boy who, instead of being quarrelsome, lives at peace with the other boys, has the Kingdom of God within him. Any boy whose heart is filled with joy because he does what is right, has the Kingdom of God within him. The Kingdom of God is not going to religious meetings, and hearing strange religious experiences; the Kingdom of God is doing what is right—living at peace with all men, being filled with joy in the Holy Ghost.

Boys, if you are going to be Christians, be Christians as boys, and not as your grandmothers. A grandmother has to be a Christian as a grandmother, and that is the right and the beautiful thing for her; but if you cannot read your Bible by the hours as your grandmother can, or delight in meetings as she can, don't think you are necessarily a bad boy. When you are your grandmother's age you will have your grandmother's kind of religion. Meantime, be a Christian as a boy. Live a boy's life. Do the straight thing; seek the kingdom of righteousness and honor and truth. Keep the peace with the boys about you, and be filled with the joy of being a loyal, and simple, and natural, and boy-like servant of Christ.

You can very easily tell a house, or a workshop, or an office where the Kingdom of God is *not*. The first thing you see in that pace is that the "straight thing" is not always done. Customers do not get fair play. You are in danger of learning to cheat and to lie. Better a thousand times to starve than to stay in a place where you cannot do what is right.

Or, when you go into your workshop, you find everybody sulky, touchy, and ill-tempered, everybody at daggers-drawn with everybody else, some of the men not on speaking terms with some of the others, and the whole *feel* of the place miserable and unhappy. The Kingdom of God is not thee, for *it* is peace. It is the Kingdom of the Devil that is anger, and wrath and malice.

If you want to get the Kingdom of God into your workshop, or into your home, let the quarreling be stopped. Live in peace and harmony and brotherliness with everyone. For the Kingdom of God is a kingdom of brothers. It is a great Society, founded by Jesus Christ, of all the people who try to live like Him, and to make the world better and sweeter and happier. Wherever boy is trying to do that, in the house or on the street, in the workshop or on the baseball field, there is the Kingdom of God. And every boy, however small or obscure or poor, who is seeking that, is a member of it. You see now, I hope, what the Kingdom is.

II. *I pass, therefore, to the second head; What was it? Arithmetic. Are there any arithmetic words in this text? "Added." What other arithmetic words? "First."*

Now, don't you think you could not have anything better to seek "first" than the things I have named to do what is right, to live at peace, and be always making those about you happy? You see at once why Christ tells us to seek these things first—because they are the best worth seeking.

Do you know anything better than these three things, anything happier, purer, nobler? If you do, seek them first. But if you do not, seek first the Kingdom of God. I do not tell you to be religious. You know that. I do not tell you to seek the Kingdom of God. I tell you to seek the Kingdom of God *first. first.* Not many people do that. They put a little religion into their life—once a week, perhaps. They might just as well let it alone. It is not worth seeking the Kingdom of God unless we seek it *first.*

Suppose you take the helm out of a ship and hang it over the bow, and send that ship to sea, will it ever reach the other side? Certainly not. It will drift about anyhow. Keep religion in its place, and it will take you straight through life and straight to your Father in heaven when life is over. But if you do not put it in its place, you may just as well have nothing to do with it. Religion out of its place in a human life is the most miserable thing in the world. There is nothing that requires so much to be kept in its place as religion, and its place is what? second? third? "First." Boys, *first* the Kingdom of God; make it so that it will be natural to you to think about that the very first thing.

There was a boy in Glasgow apprenticed to a gentleman who made telegraphs. (The gentleman told me this himself.) One day this boy was up on the top of a four-story house with a number of men fixing up a telegraph wire. The work was all but done. It was getting late, and the men said they were going away home, and the boy was to nip off the ends of the wire himself. Before going down they told him to be sure to go back to the workshop, when he was finished, with his master's tools.

"Do not leave any of them lying about, whatever you do," said the foreman.

The boy climbed up the pole and began to nip off the ends of the wire. It was a very cold winter night, and the dusk was gathering. He lost his hold and fell upon the slates, slid down, and then over and over to the ground below. A clothes-rope stretched across the "green" on which he was just about to fall, caught him on the chest and broke his fall; but the shock was terrible, and he lay unconscious among some clothes upon the green.

An old woman came out; seeing her rope broken and the clothes all soiled, thought the boy was drunk, shook him, scolded him, and went for the policeman. The boy with the shaking came back to consciousness, rubbed his eyes, and got back on his feet. What do you think he did? He staggered, half-blind, up the stairs. He climbed the ladder. He got on to the roof of the house. He gathered up his tools, put them into his basket, took them down, and when he got to the ground again fainted dead away.

Just then the policeman came, saw there was something seriously wrong, and carried him away to the hospital, where he lay for some time. I am glad to say he got better.

What was his first thought at that terrible moment? His duty. He was not thinking of himself; he was thinking about his master. First, the Kingdom of God.

But there is another arithmetic word. What is it? "Added."

You know the difference between *addition* and *subtraction*. Now, that is a very important difference in religion, because—and it is a very strange thing—very few people know the difference when they begin to talk about religion. They often tell boys that if they seek the Kingdom of God, everything else is going to be *subtracted* from them. They tell them that they are going to become gloomy, miserable, and will lose everything that makes a boy's life worth living—that they will have to stop baseball and story-books, and become little old men, and spend all their time in going to meetings and in singing hymns.

Now, that is not true. Christ never said anything like that. Christ said we are to "Seek first the Kingdom of God," and everything else worth having is to be *added* unto us. If there is anything I would like you to remember, it is these two arithmetic words—"first" and "added."

I do not mean by "added" that if you become religious you are all going to become *rich*. Here is a boy, who, in sweeping out the shop tomorrow, finds a quarter lying among the orange boxes. Well, nobody has missed it. He puts it in his pocket, and it begins to burn a hole there. by breakfast time he wishes that money were in his master's pocket. And by-and-by he goes to his master. He says (to *himself,* and not to his master), "I was at the Boys' Brigade yesterday and I was told to seek *first* that which was right." Then he says to his master:

"Please, sir, here is a quarter that I found upon the floor."

The master puts it in the till. What has the boy got in his pocket? Nothing; *but he has got the kingdom of God in his heart.* He has laid up treasure in heaven, which is of infinitely more worth than the quarter.

Now, that boy does not find a dollar on his way home. I have known that to happen, but that is not what is meant by "adding." It does not mean that God is going to pay him in his own coin, for He pays in better coin.

Yet I remember once hearing of a boy who was paid in both ways. He was very, very poor. He lived in a foreign country, and his mother said to him one day that he must go into the great city and start in business, and she took his coat and cut it open and sewed between the lining and the coat forty golden dinars, which she had saved up for many years to start him in life. She told him to take care of robbers as he went across the desert; and as he was going out of the door she said:

"My boy, I have only two words for you—'Fear God, and never tell a lie.'"

The boy started off, and towards evening he saw glittering in the distance the minarets of the great city. But between the city and himself he saw a cloud of dust. It came nearer. Presently he saw that it was a band of robbers.

One of the robbers left the rest and rode toward him, and said:

"Boy, what have you got?"

The boy looked him in the face and said:

"I have forty golden dinars sewed up in my coat."

it by our Captain. Now, there is His command to seek *first* the Kingdom of God. Have you done it?

"Well," I know some boys will say, "we are going to have a good time, enjoy life, and then we are going to seek—*last*—the Kingdom of God."

Now, that is mean; it is nothing else than mean for a boy to take all the good gifts that God has given him, and then give him nothing back in return but his wasted life.

God wants boys' *lives,* not only their souls. It is for active, service that soldiers are drilled, and trained, and fed, and armed. That is why you and I are in the world at all—not to prepare to go out of it some day, but to serve God actively in it *now.* It is monstrous, and shameful, and cowardly to talk of seeking the Kingdom *last.* It is shirking duty, abandoning one's rightful post, playing into the enemy's hand by doing nothing to turn his flank. Every hour a Kingdom is coming in your heart, in your home, in the world near you, be it a Kingdom of Darkness or a Kingdom of Light. You are placed where you are, in a particular business, in a particular street, to help on there the Kingdom of God. You cannot do that when you are old and ready to die. By that time your companions will have fought their fight, and lost or won. If they lose, will you not be sorry that you did not help them? Will you not regret that only at the last you helped the Kingdom of God? Perhaps you will not be able to do it then. And then your life has been lost indeed.

Very few people have the opportunity to seek the Kingdom of God at the end. Christ, knowing all that, knowing that religion was a thing for our life, not merely for our death-bed, has laid this command upon us now: "Seek *first* the Kingdom of God."

I am going to leave you with this text itself. Every boy in the world should obey it.

Boys, before you go to work to-morrow, before you go to sleep to-night, resolve that, God helping you, you are going to seek *first* the Kingdom of God. Perhaps some boys here are deserters; they began once before to serve Christ, and they deserted. Come back again, come back again today! Others have never enlisted at all. Will you not do it now? You are old enough to decide. The grandest moment of a boy's life is that moment when he decides to *"seek first the Kingdom of God."*

The Changed Life:
The Greatest Need of the World.

God is all for quality; man is for quantity. The immediate need of the world at this moment is not more of us, but, if I may use the expression, a better brand of us. To secure ten men of an improved type would be better than if we had ten thousand more of the average Christians distributed all over the world. There is such a thing in the evangelistic sense as winning the whole world and losing our own soul. And the first consideration of our own life—our own spiritual relations to God—our own likeness to Christ. And I am anxious, briefly, to look at the right and the wrong way of becoming like Christ—of becoming better men: the right and the wrong way of sanctification.

Let me begin by naming, and in part discarding some processes in vogue already for producing better lives. These processes are far from wrong; in their place they may even be essential. One ventures to disparage them only because they do not turn out the most perfect possible work.

1.　　The first imperfect method is to rely on resolution. In will power, in mere spasms of earnestness, there is no salvation. Struggle, effort, even agony, have their place in Christianity, as we shall see; but this is not where they come in.

In mid-Atlantic the Etruria, in which I was sailing, suddenly stopped. Something had gone wrong with the engines. There were five hundred able-bodied men on board the ship. Do you think that if we had gathered together and pushed against the mast we could have pushed it on?

When one attempts to sanctify himself by effort, he is trying to make his boat go by pushing against the mast. He is like a drowning man trying to lift himself out of the water by pulling at the hair of his own head.

Christ held up this method almost to ridicule when He said, "Which of you by taking thought can add a cubit to his stature?" Put down that method forever as being futile.

The one redeeming feature of the self-sufficient method is this—that those who try it find out almost at once that it will not gain the goal.

2.   Another experimenter says: "But that is not my method. I have seen the folly of a mere wild struggle in the dark. I work on a principle. My plan is not to waste power on random effort, but to concentrate on a single sin. By taking one at a time and crucifying it steadily, I hope in the end to extirpate all."

To this, unfortunately, there are four objections: For one thing, life is too short; the name of sin is legion. For another thing, to deal with individual sins is to leave the rest of the nature for the time untouched. In the third place, a single combat with a special sin does not affect the root and spring of the disease. If you dam up a stream at one place, it will simply overflow higher up. If only one of the channels of sin be obstructed, experience points to an almost certain overflow through some other part of the nature. Partial conversion is almost always accompanied by such moral leakage, for the pent-up energies accumulate to the bursting point, and the last state of that soul may be worse than the first. In the last place, religion does not consist in negatives, in stopping this sin and stopping that. The perfect character can never be produced with a pruning knife.

3.   But a third protests: "So be it. I make no attempt to stop sins one by one. My meth od is just the opposite. I copy the virtues one by one."

The difficulty about the copying method is that it is apt to be mechanical. One can always tell an engraving from a picture, an artificial flower from a real flower. To copy virtues one by one has somewhat the same effect as eradicating the vices one by one; the temporary result is an overbalanced and incongruous character. Some one defines a *prig* as "a creature that is over-fed for its size." One sometimes finds Christians of this species—over-fed on one side of their nature, but dismally thin and starved looking on the other. The result, for instance, of copying Humility, and adding it on to an otherwise worldly life, is simply grotesque. A rabid temperance advocate, for the same reason, is often the poorest of creatures, flourishing on a single virtue, and quite oblivious that his Temperance is making a worse man of him and not a better. These are examples of fine virtues spoiled by association with mean companions. Character is a unity, and all the virtues must advance together to make the perfect man.

This method of sanctification, nevertheless, is in the true direction. It is only in the details of execution that it fails.

4   A fourth method I need scarcely mention, for it is a variation on those already named. It is the very young man's method, and the pure earnestness of it makes it almost desecration to touch it. It is to keep

a private note-book with columns for the days of the week, and a list of virtues, with spaces against each for marks. this, with many stern rules for preface, is stored away in a secret place, and from time to time, at nightfall, the soul is arraigned before it as before a private judgment bar.

This living by code was Franklin's method; and I suppose thousands more could tell how they had hung up in their bedrooms, or hid in locked-fast drawers, the rules which one solemn day they drew up to shape their lives.

This method is not erroneous, only somehow its success is poor. You bear me witness that it fails. And it fails generally for very matter-of-fact reasons—most likely because one day we forget the rules.

All these methods that have been named—the self-sufficient method, the self-crucifixion method, the mimetic method, and the diary method—are perfectly human, perfectly natural, perfectly ignorant, and as they stand perfectly inadequate. It is not argued, I repeat, that they must be abandoned. Their harm is rather that they distract attention from the true working method, and secure a fair result at the expense of the perfect one. What that perfect method is we shall now go on to ask.

I. THE FORMULA OF SANCTIFICATION.

A formula, a receipt for Sanctification—can one seriously speak of this mighty change as if the process were as definite as for the production of so many volts of electricity?

It is impossible to doubt it. Shall a mechanical experiment succeed infallibly, and the one vital experiment of humanity remain a chance? Is corn to grow by method, and character by caprice? If we cannot calculate to a certainty that the forces of religion will do their work, then is religion vain. And if we cannot

race. Even physiologically he is a mirror. His second sentence records that he is a politician, and a faint reflection in the way he pronounces *the times* reveals his party. In his next remarks I see reflected a whole world of experiences. The books he has read, the people he has met, the companions he keeps, the influences that have played upon him and made him the man he is—these are all registered there by a pen which lets nothing pass, and whose writing can never be blotted out.

What I am reading in him meantime he is also reading in me; and before the journey is over we could half write each other's lives. Whether we like it or not, we live in glass houses. The mind, the memory, the soul, is simply a vast chamber paneled with looking-glass. And upon this miraculous arrangement and endowment depends the capacity of mortal souls to "reflect the character of the Lord."

(2) But this is not all. If all these varied reflections from our so-called secret life are patent to the world, how close the writing, complete the record within the soul itself! For the influences we meet are not simply held for a moment on the polished surface and thrown off again into space. Each is retained where first it fell, and stored up in the soul forever.

This law of assimilation is the second, and by far the most impressive truth which underlies the formula of sanctification—the truth that men are not only mirrors, but that these mirrors, so far from being mere reflectors of the fleeting things they see, transfer into their own inmost substance, and hold in permanent preservation the things that they reflect.

No one knows how the soul can hold these things. No one knows how the miracle is done. No phenomenon in nature, no process in chemistry, no chapter in necromancy can ever help us to begin to understand this amazing operation. For, think of it, the past is not only

focused there, in a man's soul, it *is* there. How could it
be reflected from there if it were not there? All things
that he has ever seen, known, felt, believed of the surrounding world are now within him, have become part
of him, in part are him—he has been changed into their
image. He may deny it, he may resent it, but they are
there. They do not adhere to him, they are transfused
through him. He cannot alter or rub them out. They
are not in his memory, they are in *him*. His soul is as
they have filled it, made it, left it. These things, these
books, these events, these influences are his makers.
In their hands are life and death, beauty and deformity.
When once the image or likeness of any of these is fairy
presented to the soul, no power on earth can hinder
two things happening—it must be absorbed into the
soul and forever reflected back again from character.

Upon these astounding yet perfectly obvious psy-
chological facts, Paul bases his doctrine of sanctification. He sees that character is a thing built up by slow
degrees, that it is hourly changing for better or for
worse according to the images which flit across it. One
step further and the whole length and breadth of the
application of these ideas to the central problem of religion will stand before us.

II. THE ALCHEMY OF INFLUENCE.

If events change men, much more persons. No man
can meet another on the street without making some
mark upon him. We say we exchange words when we
meet; what we exchange is souls. And when intercourse
is very close and very frequent, so complete is this exchange that recognizable bits of the one soul begin to
show in the other's nature, and the second is conscious
of a similar and growing debt to the first.

Now, we become like those whom we habitually reflect. I could prove from science that applies even to
the physical framework of animals—that they are in-

fluenced and organically changed by the environment in which they life.

This mysterious approximating of two souls, who has not witnessed? Who has not watched some old couple come down life's pilgrimage hand in hand, with such gentle trust and joy in one another that their very faces wore the self-same look? These were not two souls; it was a composite soul. It did not matter to which of the two you spoke, you would have said the same words to either. It was quite indifferent which replied, each would have said the same. Half a century's *reflecting* had told upon them; they were changed into the same image. It is the Law of Influence that *we become like those whom we habitually reflect:* these had become like because they habitually reflected. Through all the range of literature, of history, and biography this law presides. Men are all mosaics of other men. There was a savor of David about Jonathan, and a savor of Jonathan about David. Metempsychosis is a fact. George Eliot's message to the world was that men and women make men and women. The Family, the cradle of mankind, has no meaning apart from this. Society itself is nothing but a rallying point for these omnipotent forces to do their work. On the doctrine of Influence, in short, the whole vast pyramid of humanity is built.

But it was reserved for Paul to make the supreme application of the Law of Influence. It was a tremendous inference to make, but he never hesitated. He himself was a changed man; he knew exactly what had done it; *It was Christ.*

On the Damascus road they met, and from that hour his life was absorbed in His. The effect could not but follow—on words, on deeds, on career, on creed. The "impressed forces" did their vital work. He became like Him Whom he habitually loved. "So we all," he writes, "reflecting as a mirror the glory of Christ, are changed into the same image."

Nothing could be more simple, more intelligible, more natural, more supernatural. It is an analogy from an every-day fact. Since we are what we are by the impacts of those who surround us, those who surround themselves with the highest will be those who change into the highest. There are some men and some women in whose company we are always at our best. While with them we cannot think mean thoughts or speak ungenerous words. Their mere presence is elevation, purification, sanctity. All the best stops in our nature are drawn out by their intercourse, and we find a music in our souls that was never there before. Suppose even *that* influence prolonged through a month, a year, a lifetime, and what could not life become? There, even on the common plane of life, talking our language, walking our streets, working side by side, are sanctifiers of souls; here, breathing through common clay, is Heaven; here, energies charged even through a temporal medium with the virtue of regeneration. If to live with men, diluted to the millionth degree with the virtue of the Highest, can exalt and purify the nature, what bounds can be set to the influence of Christ? To live with Socrates—with unveiled face—must have made one wise; with Aristides, just. Francis Assisi must have made one gentle; Savonarola, strong. But to have lived with Christ must have made one like Christ: that is to say, A *Christian*.

As a matter of fact, to live with Christ did produce this effect. It produced it in the case of Paul. And during Christ's lifetime the experiment was tried in an even more startling form. A few raw, unspiritual, uninspiring men, were admitted to the inner circle of His friendship. The change began at once. Day by day we can almost see the first disciple grow. First there steals over them the faintest possible adumbration of His character, and occasionally, very occasionally, they do a thing or say a thing that they could not have done or said had they not been living there. Slowly the spell of His Life deepens. Reach after reach of their nature is overtaken, thawed, subjugated, sanctified. Their manner softens, their words become more gentle, their conduct more unselfish. As swallows who have found a summer, as frozen buds the spring, their starved humanity bursts into a fuller life. They do not know how it is, but they are different men.

One day they find themselves like their Master, going about and doing good. To themselves it is unaccountable, but they cannot do otherwise. they were not told to do it, it came to them to do it. But the people who watch them know well how to account for it—"They have been," they whisper, "with Jesus." Already even, the mark and seal of His character is upon them—"They have been with Jesus." Unparalleled phenomenon, that these poor fishermen should remind other men of Christ! Stupendous victory and mystery of regeneration that mortal men should suggest *god* to the world!

There is something almost melting in the way his contemporaries, and John especially, speak of the influence of Christ. John lived himself in daily wonder at Him; he was overpowered, over-awed, entranced, transfigured. To his mind it was impossible for any one to come under this influence and ever be the same again. "Whosoever abideth in Him sinneth not," he said. It was inconceivable that he should sin, as inconceivable as that ice should live in a burning sun, or darkness coexist with noon. If any one did sin, it was to John the simple proof that he could never have met Christ. "Whosoever sinneth," he exclaims, "hath not seen *him*, neither known *him*." Sin was abashed in this

Presence. Its root withered. Its sway and victory were forever at an end.

But these were His contemporaries. It was easy for *them* to be influenced by Him, for they were every day and all the day together. But how can we mirror that which we have never seen? How can all this stupendous result be produced by a Memory, by the scantiest of all Biographies, by One who lived and left this earth eighteen hundred years ago? How can modern men to-day make Christ, the absent Christ, their most constant companion still?

The answer is that Friendship is a spiritual thing.

It is independent of Matter, or Space, or Time. That which I love in my friend is not that which I see. What influences me in my friend is not his body but his spirit. He influences me about as much in his absence as in his presence. It would have been an ineffable experience truly to have lived at that time—

> "I think when I read the sweet story of old,
> How when Jesus was here among men,
> He took little children like lambs to his fold,
> I should like to have been with Him then.
>
> "I wish that His hand had been laid on my head,
> That His arms had been thrown around me,
> And that I had seen His kind look when he said,
> 'Let the little ones come unto me.'"

And yet, if Christ were to come into the world again, few of us probably would ever have a chance of seeing Him. Millions of her subjects in the little country of England have never seen their own Queen. And there would be millions of the subjects of Christ who could never get within speaking distance of Him if He were here. We remember He said: "It is expedient for you (not *for me*) that I go away"; because by going away He could really be nearer to us than He would have been if He had stayed here. It would be geographically and physically impossible for most of us to be influenced by His person had He remained. And so our communion with Him is a spiritual companionship; but not different from most companionships, which, when you press them down to the roots, you will find to be essentially spiritual.

All friendship, all love, human and Divine, is purely spiritual. It was after He was risen that He influenced even the disciples most. Hence, in reflecting the character of Christ, it is no real obstacle that we may never have been in visible contact with Himself.

There lived once a young girl whose perfect grace of character was the wonder of those who knew her. She wore on her neck a gold locket which no one was ever allowed to open. One day, in a moment of unusual confidence, one of her companions was allowed to touch its spring and learn its secret. She saw written these words—*"Whom having not seen I love."*

That was the secret of her beautiful life. She had been changed into the Same Image.

Now this is not imitation, but a much deeper thing. Mark this distinction, for the difference in the process as well as in the result, may be as great as that between a photograph secured by the infallible pencil of the sun, and the rude outline from a school-boy's chalk. Imitation is mechanical, reflection organic. The one is occasional, the other habitual. In the one case, man comes to God and imitates him; in the other, God comes to man and imprints Himself upon him. It is quite true that there is an imitation of Christ which amounts to reflection. But Paul's term includes all that the other holds, and is open to no mistake.

What, then, is the practical lesson? It is obvious. "Make Christ your most constant companion"—this is what it practically means for us. Be more under His influences than under any other influence. Ten minutes spent in His society every day, ay, two minutes if it be face to face, and heart to heart, will make the whole day different. Every character has an inward spring,—let Christ be it. Every action has a key-note,— let Christ set it.

Yesterday you got a certain letter. You sat down and wrote a reply which almost scorched the paper. You picked the cruelest adjectives you knew and sent it forth, without a pang to do its ruthless work. You did that because your life was set in the wrong key. You began the day with the mirror placed at the wrong angle.

Tomorrow at day-break, turn it towards Him, and even to your enemy the fashion of your countenance will be changed. Whatever you then do, one thing you will find you could not do—you could not write that letter. Your first impulse may be the same, your judgement may be unchanged, but if you try it the ink will dry on your pen, and you will rise from your desk an unavenged, but greater and more Christian man. Throughout the whole day your actions, down to the last detail, will do homage to that early vision.

Yesterday you thought mostly about yourself. Today the poor will meet you, and you will feed them. The helpless, the tempted, the sad, will throng about you, and each you will befriend. Where were all these people yesterday? Where they are today, but you did not see them. It is in reflected light that the poor are seen. But your soul today is not at the ordinary angle.

"Things which are not seen" are visible. For a few short hours you live the Eternal Life. The eternal life, the life of faith, is simply the life of a higher vision. Faith is an attitude—a mirror set at the right angle.

When tomorrow is over, and in the evening you review it, you will wonder how you did it. You will not be conscious that you strove for anything, or imitated anything, or crucified anything. You will be conscious of Christ; that He was with you, that without compulsion you were yet compelled; that without force, or noise, or proclamation, the revolution was accomplished. You do not congratulate yourself as one who has done a mighty deed, or achieved a personal success, or stored up a fund of "Christian experience" to ensure the same result again. What you are conscious of is "the glory of the Lord." And what the world is conscious of, if the result be a true one, is also "the glory of the Lord." In looking at a mirror one does not see the mirror, or think of it, but only of what it reflects. For a mirror never calls the attention to itself—except when there are flaws in it.

Let me say a word or two more about the effects which necessarily must follow from this contact, or fellowship, with Christ. I need not quote the texts upon the subject—the texts about abiding in Christ. "He that abideth in Him sinneth not." You cannot sin when you are standing in front of Christ. You simply cannot do it. Again: "If ye abide in Me, and My words abide in you, ye shall ask what ye will, and it shall be done unto you." Think of that! That is another inevitable consequence. And there is yet another: "He that abideth in Me, the same bringeth forth much fruit." Sinlessness—answered prayer—much fruit.

But in addition to these things, see how many of the highest Christian virtues and experiences necessarily flow from the assumption of that attitude towards Christ. For instance, the moment you assume that relation to Christ you begin to know what the *child-spirit* is. You stand before Christ, and He becomes your Teacher, and you instinctively become docile. Then you learn also to become *charitable* and *tolerant*; because you are learning of Him, and He is "meek and lowly in heart," and you catch that spirit. That is a bit of His character being reflected into yours. Instead of being critical and self-asserting, you become humble and have the mind of a little child.

I think, further, the only way of learning what *faith* is is to know Christ and be in His company. You hear sermons about the nine different kinds of faith—distinctions drawn between the right kind of faith and the wrong—and sermons telling you how to get faith. So far as I can see, there is only one way in which faith is got, and it is the same in the religious world as it is in the world of men and women. I learn to trust you, my brother, just as I get to trust me just as you get to know me. I do not trust you as a stranger, but as I come into contact with you, and watch you, and live with you, I find out that you are trustworthy, and I come to trust myself to you, and to lean upon you. But I do not do that to a stranger.

The way to trust Christ is to know Christ. You cannot help trusting Him them. You are changed. By knowing Him faith is begotten in you, as cause and effect. To trust Him without knowing Him as thousands do, is not faith, but credulity. I believe a great deal of prayer for faith is thrown away. What we should pray for is that we may be able to fulfill the condition, and when we have fulfilled the condition, the faith necessarily follows. The way, therefore, to increase our faith is to increase our intimacy with Christ. We trust Him more and more the better we know Him.

And then another immediate effect of this way of sanctifying the character is the tranquility that it brings over the Christian life. How disturbed and distressed and anxious Christian people are about their growth in grace! Now, the moment you give that over into Christ's care—the moment you see that you are *being* changed—that anxiety passes away. You see that it must follow by an inevitable process and by a natural law if you fulfill the simple condition; so that peace is the reward of that life and fellowship with Christ.

Many other things follow. A man's usefulness depends to a large extent upon his fellowship with Christ. That is obvious. Only Christ can influence the world; but all that the world sees of Christ is what it sees of you and me. Christ said: "The world seeth Me no more, but ye see Me." You see Him, and standing in front of Him reflect Him, and the world sees the reflection. It cannot see Him. So that a Christian's usefulness depends solely upon that relationship.

Now, I have only pointed out a few of the things that follow from the standing before Christ—from the abiding in Christ. You will find, if you run over the texts about abiding in Christ, many other things will suggest themselves in the same relations. Almost everything in Christian experience and character follows and follows necessarily, from standing before Christ and reflecting his character. But the supreme consummation is that we are changed into *the same image,* "even as by the Lord the Spirit." That is to say that in some way, unknown to us, but possibly not more mysterious than the doctrine of personal influence, we are changed into the image of Christ.

This method cannot fail. I am not setting before you an opinion or a theory, but this is a certainly successful means of sanctification. "We all, with unveiled face, reflecting in a mirror the glory of Christ (the character of Christ) assuredly—without any miscarriage—without any possibility of miscarriage—are changed into the same image." It is an immense thing to be anchored in some great principle like that. Emerson says: "The hero is the man who is immovably centered." Get immovably centered in that doctrine of sanctification. Do not be carried away by the hundred and one theories of sanctification that are floating about in religious literature of the country at the present time; but go to the bottom of the thing for yourself, and see the *rationale* of it for yourself, and you will come to see that it is a matter of cause and effect, and that if you will fulfill the condition laid down by Christ, the effect must follow by a natural law.

What a prospect! To be changed into the same image. Think of that! That is what we are here for. That is what we are elected for. Not to be saved, in the common acceptation, but "whom He did foreknow He also did predestinate to be conformed to the image of His Son." Not merely to be saved, but *to be conformed to the image of his son.* Conserve that principle. And as we must spend time in cultivating our earthly friendships if we are to have their blessings, so we must spend time in cultivating the fellowship and companionship of Christ. And there is nothing so much worth taking into our lives as a profounder sense of what is to be had by living in communion with Christ, and by getting nearer to Him. It will matter much if we take away with us some of the thoughts about theology, and some of the new light that has been shed upon the text of Scripture; it will matter infinitely more if our fellowship with the Lord Jesus become a little closer, and our theory of holy living a little more rational. And then as we go forth, men will take knowledge of us, that we have been with Jesus, and as we reflect Him upon them, they will begin to be changed into the same image.

It seems to me the preaching is of infinitely smaller account than the life which mirrors Christ. That is bound to tell; without speech or language—like the voices of the stars. It throws out its impressions on every side. The one simple thing we have to do is to be there—in the right relation; to go through life hand in hand with Him; to have Him in the room with us, and keeping us company wherever we go; to depend upon Him and lean upon Him, and so have His life reflected in the fullness of its beauty and perfection into ours.

III. THE FIRST EXPERIMENT.

Then you reduce religion to a common Friendship? A common Friendship—who talks of a *common* Friendship? There is no such thing in the world.

On earth no word is more sublime. Friendship is the nearest thing we know to what religion is. God is love. And to make religion akin to Friendship is simply to give it the highest expression conceivable by man. But if by demurring to "a common friendship" is meant a protest against the greatest and the holiest in religion being spoken of in intelligible terms, then I am afraid the objection is all to real. Men always look for a mystery when one talks of sanctification, some mystery apart from that which must ever be mysterious wherever Spirit works. It is thought some peculiar secret lies behind it, some occult experience which only the initiated know. Thousands of persons go to church every Sunday hoping to solve this mystery. At meeting, at conferences, many a time they have reached what they thought was the very brink of it, but somehow no further revelation came. Poring over religious books, how often were they not within a paragraph of it; the next page, the next sentence, would discover all, and they would be borne on a flowing tide forever. But nothing happened. The next sentence and the next page were read, and still it eluded them; and though the promise of its coming kept faithfully up to the end, the last chapter found them still pursuing.

Why did nothing happen? Because there was nothing to happen—nothing of the kind they were looking for. Why did it elude them? Because there was no "it." When shall we learn that the pursuit of holiness is simply the pursuit of Christ? When shall we substitute for the "it" of a fictitious aspiration, the approach to a Living Friend? Sanctity is in character and not in moods; Divinity in our own plain calm humanity, and in no mystic rapture of the soul.

And yet there are others who, for exactly a contrary reason, will find scant satisfaction here. Their complaint is not that a religion expressed in terms of Friendship is too homely, but that it is still too mystical. To "abide" in Christ, to "make Christ our most constant companion," is to them the purest mysticism. They want something absolutely tangible and absolutely direct. These are not the poetical souls who seek a sign, a mysticism in excess, but the prosaic natures whose want is mathematical definition in details. Yet it is perhaps not possible to reduce this problem to much more rigid elements. The beauty of Friendship is its infinity. One can never evacuate life of mysticism. Home is full of it, love is full of it, religion is full of it. Why stumble at that in the relation of man to Christ which is natural in the relation of man to man?

If any one cannot conceive or realize a mystical relation with Christ, perhaps all that can be done is to help him to step on to it by still plainer analogies from common life. How do I know Shakspere or Dante? By communing with their words and thoughts. Many men know Dante better than their own fathers. Many men know Dante better than their own fathers. He influences them more. As a spiritual presence he is more near to them, as a spiritual force more real. Is there any reason why a greater than Shakspere or Dante, who also walked this earth, who left great words behind Him, who has greater works everywhere in the world now, should not also instruct, inspire and mould the characters of men? I do not limit Christ's influence to this: it is this, and it is more. But Christ, so far from resenting or discouraging this relation of

Friendship, Himself proposed it. "Abide in me" was almost His last word to the world. And He partly met the difficulty of those who feel its intangibleness by adding the practical clause, "If ye abide in Me, *and My words abide in you.*"

Begin with His words. Words can scarcely ever be long impersonal. Christ himself was a Word, a word made Flesh. Make His words flesh; do them, live them, and you must live Christ. *"he that keepeth My commandments,* he it is that loveth Me." Obey Him and you must love Him. Abide in Him, and you must obey Him. *cultivate* His Friendship. Live after Christ, in His Spirit, as in His Presence, and it is difficult to think what more you can do. Take this at least as a first lesson, as introduction.

If you cannot at once and always feel the play of His life upon yours, watch for it also indirectly. "The whole earth is full of the character of the Lord." Christ is the Light of the world, and much of his Light is reflected from things in the world—even from clouds. Sunlight is stored in every leaf, from leaf through coal, and it comforts us thence when days are dark and we cannot see the sun. Christ shines through men, through books, through history, through nature, music, art. Look for Him there. "Every day one should either look at a beautiful picture, or hear beautiful music, or read a beautiful poem." The real danger of mysticism is not making it broad enough.

Do not think that nothing is happening because you do not see yourself grow, or hear the whir of the machinery. All great things grow noiselessly. You can see a mushroom grow, but never a child. Paul said for the comforting of all slowly perfecting souls that they grew "from character to character." "The inward man," he says elsewhere, "is renewed from day to day." All thorough work is slow; all true development by minute, slight and insensible metamorphoses. The higher the structure, moreover, the slower the progress. As the biologist runs his eye over the long Ascent of Life, he sees the lowest forms of animals develop in an hour; the next above these reach maturity in a day; those higher still take weeks or months to perfect; but the few at the top demand the long experiment of years. If a child and an ape are born on the same day, the last will be in full possession of its faculties and doing the active work of life before the child has left its cradle. Life is the cradle of eternity. As the man is to the animal in the slowness of his evolution, so is the spiritual man to the natural man. Foundations which have to bear the weight of an eternal life must be surely laid. Character is to wear forever; who will wonder or grudge that it cannot be developed in a day?

To await the growing of a soul, nevertheless, is an almost Divine act of faith. How pardonable, surely, the impatience of deformity with itself, of a consciously despicable character standing before Christ, wondering, yearning, hungering to be like that! Yet must one trust the process fearlessly and without misgiving. "The Lord the Spirit" will do His part. The tempting expedient is, in haste for abrupt or visible progress, to try some method less spiritual, or to defeat the end by watching for effects instead of keeping the eye on the Cause. A photograph prints from the negative only while exposed to the sun. While the artist is looking to see how it is getting on he simply stops the getting on. Whatever of wise supervision the soul may need, it is certain it can never be over-exposed, or that, being exposed, anything else in the world can improve the result or quicken it. The creation of a new heart, the renewing of a right spirit, is an omnipotent work of God. Leave it to the Creator. "He which hath begun a good work in you will perfect it unto that day."

No man, nevertheless, who feels the worth and solemnity of what is at stake will be careless as to his progress. To become like Christ is the only thing in the world worth caring for, the thing before which every ambition of man is folly, and all lower achievement vain.

Those only who make this quest the supreme desire and passion of their lives can ever begin to hope to reach it. If, therefore, it has seemed up to this point as if all depended on passivity, let me now assert, with conviction more intense, that all depends on activity. A religion of effortless adoration may be a religion for an angel, but never for a man. No in the contemplative, but in the active, lies true hope; not in rapture, but in reality, lies true life; not in the realm of ideals, but among tangible things, is man's sanctification wrought. Resolution, effort, pain, self-crucifixion, agony—all the things already dismissed as futile in themselves, must now be restored to office, and a tenfold responsibility laid upon them. For what is their office? Nothing less than to move the vast inertia of the soul, and place it, and keep it where the spiritual forces will act upon it. It is to rally the forces of the will, and keep the surface of the mirror bright and ever in position. It is to uncover the face which is to look at Christ, and draw down the veil when unhallowed sights are near.

You have, perhaps, gone with an astronomer to watch him photograph the spectrum of a star. As you enter the dark vault of the observatory you saw him being by lighting a candle. To see the star with? No; but to adjust the instrument to see the star with. It was the star that was going to take the photograph; it was, also, the astronomer. For a long time he worked in the dimness, screwing tubes and polishing lenses and adjusting reflectors, and only after much labor the finely focused instrument was brought to bear. Then he blew out the light, and left the start to do its work upon the plate alone.

The day's task for the Christian is to bring his instrument to bear. Having done that he may blow out his candle. All the evidences of Christianity which have brought him there, all aids to Faith, all acts of worship, all the leverages of the Church, all Prayer and Meditation, all girding of the Will—these lesser processes, these candle-light activities for that supreme hour, may be set aside. But, remember, it is but for an hour. The wise man will be he who quickest lights his candle; the wisest he who never lets it out. Tomorrow, the next moment, he, a poor, darkened, blurred soul, may need it again to focus the Image better, to take a mote off the lens, to clear the mirror from a breath with which the world has dulled it.

No readjustment is ever required on behalf of the Star. That is one great fixed point in this shifting universe. But *the world moves*. And each day, each hour, demands a further motion and readjustment for the soul. A telescope in an observatory follows a star by clockwork, but the clockwork of the soul is called *the will*. Hence, while the soul in passivity reflects the Image of the Lord, the Will in intense activity holds the mirror in position lest the drifting motion of the world bear it beyond the line of vision. To "follow Christ" is largely to keep the soul in such position as will allow for the motion of the earth. And this calculated counteracting of the movements of the world, this holding of the mirror exactly opposite to the Mirrored, this steadying of the faculties unerringly through cloud and earthquake, fire and sword, is the stupendous cooperating labor of the Will. It is all man's work. It is all Christ's work. In practice it is both; in theory it is both. But the wise man will say in practice, "It depends upon myself."

In the Gallerie des Beaux Arts in Paris there stands a famous statue. It was the last work of a great genius, who, like many a genius, was very poor and lived in a garret, which served as a studio and sleeping-room alike. When the statue was all but finished, one midnight a sudden frost fell upon Paris. The sculptor lay awake in the fireless room and thought of the still moist clay, thought how the water would freeze in the pores and destroy in an hour the dream of his life. So the old man rose from his couch and heaped the bed-clothes reverently round his work. In the morning when the neighbors entered the room the sculptor was dead, but the statue was saved!

The Image of Christ that is forming within us—that is life's one charge. Let every project stand aside for that. The spirit of God who brooded upon the waters thousands of years ago, is busy now creating men, within these commonplace lives of ours, in the image of God. "Till Christ be formed," no man's work is finished, no religion crowned, no life has fulfilled its end. Is the infinite task begun? When, how, are we to be different? Time cannot change men. Death cannot change men. Christ can. Wherefore *put on Christ*.

Dealing With Doubt.

There is a subject which I think workers amongst young men cannot afford to keep out of sight—I mean the subject of "Doubt." We are forced to face that subject. We have no choice. I would rather let it alone; but every day of my life I meet men who doubt, and I am quite sure that most Christian workers among men have innumerable interviews every year with men who raise skeptical difficulties about religion.

Now it becomes a matter of great practical importance that we should know how to deal wisely with these. Upon the whole, I think these are the best men in the country. I speak of my own country. I speak of the universities with which I am familiar, and I say that they men who are perplexed,—the men who come to you with serious and honest difficulties,—are the best men. They are men of intellectual honesty, and cannot allow themselves to be put to rest by words, or phrases, or traditions, or theologies, but who must get to the bottom of things for themselves. And if I am not mistaken, Christ was very fond of these men. The outsiders always interested Him, and touched

Him. The orthodox people—the Pharisees—He was much less interested in. He went with publicans and sinners—with people who were in revolt against the respectability, intellectual and religious, of the day. And following Him, we are entitled to give sympathetic consideration to those whom He loved and took trouble with.

First, *let me speak for a moment or two about the origin of doubt.*

In the first place, we are born questioners. Look at the wonderment of a little child in its eyes before it can speak. The child's great word when it begins to speak is, "Why?" Every child is full of every kind of question, about every kind of thing, that moves, and shines and changes, in the little world in which it lives.

That is the incipient doubt in the nature of man. Respect doubt for its origin. It is an inevitable thing. It is not a thing to be crushed. It is a part of man as God made him. Heresy is truth in the making, and doubt is the prelude of knowledge.

Secondly: *the world is a sphinx.*

It is a vast riddle—an unfathomable mystery; and on every side there is temptation to questioning. In every leaf, in every cell of every leaf, there are a hundred problems. There are ten good years of a man's life in investigating what is in a leaf. God has planned the world to incite men to intellectual activity.

Thirdly: *the instrument with whcih we attempt to investigate truth is impaired.*

Some say it fell, and the glass is broken. Some say prejudice, heredity, or sin, have spoiled its sight, and have blinded our eyes and deadened our ears. In any case the instruments with which we work upon truth, even in the strongest men, are feeble and inadequate to their tremendous task.

And in the fourth place, *all religious truths are doubtable.*

There is no absolute truth for any one of them. Even that fundamental truth—the existence of a God—no man can prove by reason. The ordinary proof for the existence of a God involves either an assumption, argument in a circle, or a contradiction. The impression of God is kept up by experience, not by logic. And hence, when the experimental religion of a man, of a community, or of a nation wanes, religion wanes—their idea of God grows indistinct, and that man, community or nation becomes infidel.

Bear in mind, then, that all religious truths are doubtable—even those which we hold most strongly.

What does this brief account of the origin of doubt teach us? It teaches us great intellectual humility. It teaches us sympathy and toleration with all men who venture upon the ocean of truth to find out a path through it for themselves. Do you sometimes feel yourself thinking unkind things about your fellow-students who have intellectual difficulty? I know how hard it is always to feel sympathy and toleration for them; but we must address ourselves to that most carefully and most religiously. If my brother is short-sighted I must not abuse him or speak against him; I must pity him, and if possible try to improve his sight, or to make things that he is to look at so bright that he cannot help seeing. But never let us think evil of men who do not see as we do. From the bottom of our hearts let us pity them, and let us take them by the hand and spend time and thought over them, and try to lead them to the true light.

What has been the church's treatment of doubt in the past? It has been very simple. "There is a heretic. Burn him!" That is all. "There is a man who has gone off the road. Bring him back and torture him!"

We have got past that physically; have we got past it morally? What does the modern Church say to a man who is skeptical? Not "Burn him!" but "Brand him!" "Brand him!"—call him a bad name. And in many countries at the present time, a man who is branded as a heretic is despised, tabooed and put out of religious society, much more than if he had gone wrong in morals. I think I am speaking within the facts when I say that a man who is unsound is looked upon in many communities with more suspicion and with more pious horror than a man who now and then gets drunk. "Burn him!" "Brand him!" "Excommunicate him!" That has been the Church's treatment of doubt, and that is perhaps to some extent the treatment which we ourselves are inclined to give to the men who cannot see the truths of Christianity as we see them.

Contrast Christ's treatment of doubt. I have spoken already of His strange partiality for the outsiders—for the scattered heretics up and down the country; of the care with which He loved to deal with them, and of the respect in which He held their intellectual difficulties. Christ never failed to distinguish between doubt and unbelief. Doubt is *"can't believe"*; unbelief is *"won't believe."* Doubt is honesty; unbelief is obstinacy. Doubt is looking for light; unbelief is content with darkness. Loving darkness rather than light—that is what Christ attacked, and attacked unsparingly. But for the intellectual questioning of Thomas, and Philip, and Nicodemus, and the many others who came to Him to have their great problems solved, He was respectful and generous and tolerant.

And how did He meet their doubts? The Church, as I have said, says, "Brand him!" Christ said, "Teach him." He destroyed by fulfilling. When Thomas came to Him and denied His very resurrection, and stood before

Him waiting for the scathing words and lashing for his unbelief, they never came. They never came! Christ gave him facts—facts! No men can go around facts. Christ said, "Behold My hands and My feet." The great god of science at the present time is a fact. It words with facts. Its cry is, "Give me facts. Found anything you like upon facts and we will believe it." The spirit of Christ was the scientific spirit. He founded His religion upon facts; and He asked all men to found their religion upon facts.

Now, get up the facts of Christianity, and take men to the facts. Theologies—and I am not speaking disrespectfully of theology; theology is as scientific a thing as any other science of facts—but theologies are human versions of Divine truths, and hence the varieties of the versions and the inconsistencies of them. I would allow a man to select whichever version of this truth he liked afterwards; but I would ask him to begin with no version, but go back to the facts and base his Christian life upon these.

That is the great lesson of the New Testament way of looking at doubt—of Christ's treatment of doubt. It is not "Brand him!"—but lovingly, wisely and tenderly to teach him. Faith is never opposed to reason in the New Testament; it is opposed to sight. You will find that a principle worth thinking over. *Faith is never opposed to reason in the New Testament, but to sight.*

With these principles in mind as to the origin of doubt, as to Christ's treatment of it, how are we ourselves to deal with those who are in intellectual difficulty?

In the first place, I think *we must make all the concessions to them that we conscientiously can.*

When a doubter first encounters you, he pours out a deluge of abuse of churches, and ministers, and creeds, and Christians. Nine-tenths of what he says is probably true. Make concessions. Agree with him. It does him good to unburden himself of these things. He has been cherishing them for years—laying them up against Christians, against the Church, and against Christianity; and now he is startled to find the first Christian with whom he has talked over the thing almost entirely agrees with him. We are, of course, not responsible for everything that is said in the name of Christianity; and now he is startled to find the first Christian with whom he has talked over the thing almost entirely agrees with him. We are, of course, not responsible for everything that is said in the name of Christianity; but a man does not give up medicine because there are quack doctors, and no man has a right to give up his Christianity because there are spurious or inconsistent Christians. Then, as I already said, creeds are human versions of Divine truths; and we do not ask a man to accept all the creeds, any more than we ask him to accept all the Christians. We ask him to accept Christ, and the facts about Christ and the words of Christ. You will find the battle is half won when you have endorsed the man's objections, and possibly added a great many more to the charges which he has against ourselves. These men are in revolt against the kind of religion which we exhibit to the world—against the cant that is taught in the name of Christianity. And if the men that have never seen the real thing— if you could show them that, they would receive it as eagerly as you do. They are merely in revolt against the imperfections and inconsistencies of those who represent Christ to the world.

Second: *Beg them to set aside, by an act of will, all unsolved problems:* such as the problem of the origin of evil, the problem of the Trinity, the problem of the relation of human will and predestination, and so on—problems which have been investigated for thousands of years without result—ask them to set those problems aside as insoluble. In the meantime, just as a man who is studying mathematics may be asked to set aside the problem of squaring the circle, let him go on with what can be done, and what has been done, and leave out of sight the impossible.

You will find that will relieve the skeptic's mind of a great deal of unnecessary cargo that has been in his way.

Thirdly: *Talking about difficulties, as a rule, only aggravates them.*

Entire satisfaction to the intellect is unattainable about any of the greater problems, and if you try to get to the bottom of them by argument, there is no bottom there; and therefore you make the matter worse. But I would say what is known, and what can be honestly and philosophically and scientifically said about one or two of the difficulties that the doubter raises, just to show him that you can do it—to show him that you are not a fool—that you are not merely groping in the dark yourself, but you have found whatever basis is possible. But I would not go around all the doctrines. I would simply do that with one or two; because the moment you cut off one, a hundred other heads will grow in its place. It would be a pity if all these problems could be solved. The joy of the intellectual life would be largely gone. I would not rob a man of his problems, nor would I have another man rob me of my problems. They are the delight of life, and the whole intellectual world would be stale and unprofitable if we knew everything.

Fourthly—and this is the great point: *Turn away from the reason and go into the man's moral life.*

I don't mean, go into his moral life and see if the man is living in conscious sin, which is the great blinder of the eyes—I am speaking now of honest doubt; but open a new door into the practical side of man's nature. Entreat him not to postpone life and his life's usefulness until he has settled the problems of the universe. Tell him those problems will never all be settled; that his life will be done before he has begun to settle them; and ask him what he is doing with his life meantime. Charge him with wasting his life and his usefulness; and invite him to deal with the moral and practical difficulties of the world, and leave the intellectual difficulties as he goes along. To spend time upon these is proving the less important before the more important; and, as the French say, "The good is the enemy of the best." It is a good thing to think; it is a better thing to work—it is a better thing to do good. And you have him there, you see. He can't get beyond that. You have to tell him, in fact that there are two organs of knowledge: the one reason, the other obedience. And now tell him there is but One, and lead him to the great historical figure who calls all men to Him: the one perfect life—the one Savior of mankind—the one Light of the world. Ask him to begin to obey Christ; and, doing His will, he shall now of the doctrine whether it be of God.

That, I think, is about the only thing you can do with a man: to get him into practical contact with the needs of the world, and to let him lose his intellectual difficulties meantime. Don't ask him to give them up altogether. Tell him to solve them afterward one by one if he can, but meantime to give his life to Christ and his time to the kingdom of God. You fetch him completely around when you do that. You have taken him away from the false side of his nature, and to the practical and moral side of his nature; and for the first time in his life, perhaps, he puts things in their true place. He puts his nature in the relations in which it ought to be, and he then only begins to live. And by obedience he will soon become a learner and pupil for himself, and Christ will teach him things, and he will find whatever problems are solvable gradually solved as he goes along the path of practical duty.

Now, let me, in closing, give an instance of how to deal with specific points.

The question of miracles is thrown at my head every second day:

"What do you say to a man when he says to you, 'Why do you believe in miracles?'"

I say, "Because I have seen then."

He asks, "When?"

I say, "Yesterday."

"Where?"

"Down such-and-such a street I saw a man who was a drunkard redeemed by the power of an unseen Christ and saved from sin. That is a miracle."

The best apologetic for Christianity is a Christian. That is a fact which the man cannot get over. There are fifty other arguments for miracles, but none so good as that you have seen them. Perhaps, you are one yourself. But take a man and show him a miracle with his own eyes. Then he will believe.

The End

www.ingramcontent.com/pod-product-compliance
Lightning Source LLC
Chambersburg PA
CBHW021203020426
42331CB00003B/180